The Great Realizations

The Great Realizations
*A Commentary on the Eight Realizations
of a Bodhisattva Sutra*

Venerable Master Hsing Yun

Translated by Tom Graham

Published by Buddha's Light Publishing, Los Angeles

© 2001, 2010 Buddha's Light Publishing
First edition 2001, published as
Buddhism: Pure and Simple by Weatherhill, Inc.
Second edition 2010

By Venerable Master Hsing Yun
Translated by Tom Graham
Cover designed by Wilson Yau
Cover photograph by Chih-cheng Chang
Book designed by Amanda Ling

Published by Buddha's Light Publishing
3456 S. Glenmark Drive,
Hacienda Heights, CA 91745, U.S.A.
Tel: (626) 923-5144
Fax: (626) 923-5145
E-mail: itc@blia.org
Website: www.blpusa.com

Protected by copyright under the terms of the International Copyright Union; all rights reserved. Except for fair use in book reviews, no part of this book may be reproduced for any reason by any means, including any method of photographic reproduction, without permission of the publisher.

Printed in Taiwan.

Library of Congress Cataloging-in-Publication Data
Xingyun, da shi.
[Ba da ren jue jing. English]
The Great realizations : a commentary on the Eight Realizations of a
Bodhisattva Sutra / Venerable Master Hsing Yun ; translated by Tom Graham. — 2nd ed.
  p. cm.
Previous ed. published as: Buddhism : pure and simple. 2001.
ISBN 978-1-932293-44-9 (hardcover)
1. Ba da ren jue jing—Commentaries. I. Graham, Tom, 1951- II. Title.

BQ1529.5.P347X56 2010
294.3'823—dc22

2010007521

Contents

The Eight Realizations of a Bodhisattva Sutra 1

Introduction 7
An Overview of the Sutra

Chapter One 17
The First Realization:
The Nature of This World

Chapter Two 45
The Second Realization:
Greed is the Cause of Suffering

Chapter Three 59
The Third Realization:
Contentment is the Source of Happiness

Chapter Four 69
The Fourth Realization:
Laziness Leads to Downfall

Chapter Five. 83
The Fifth Realization:
Study Widely, Listen More

Chapter Six. 99
The Sixth Realization:
The Importance of Practicing Giving

Chapter Seven 113
The Seventh Realization:
Morality Fosters Self-control

Chapter Eight. 125
The Eighth Realization:
The Mahayana Mind

Chapter Nine 135
Conclusion:
Approaching the Awakened State

Acknowledgements

We received a lot of help from many people and we want to thank them for their efforts in making the publication of this book possible. We especially appreciate Venerable Tzu Jung, the Chief Executive of the Fo Guang Shan International Translation Center (F.G.S.I.T.C.), Venerable Hui Chi, Abbot of Hsi Lai Temple, and Venerable Yi Chao, Director of F.G.S.I.T.C. for their support and leadership; Tom Graham for his translation; Louvenia Ortega for her editing; John Gill, Nathan Michon, Amanda Ling and Wan Kah Ong for proofreading and preparing the manuscript for publication; and Wilson Yau for his cover design. Our appreciation also goes to everyone who has supported this project from its conception to its completion.

Sutra

The Eight Realizations of a Bodhisattva Sutra

The Eight Realizations of a Bodhisattva Sutra

For all disciples of the Buddha,
Each morning and night,
Recite with a sincere mind,
These eight realizations of a bodhisattva.

First, realize that this world is impermanent and that nations are dangerous and fragile. The four great elements lead to suffering and are empty and the five aggregates are without a self. All things arise, cease, change, and become different; they are illusory, not real, and cannot be controlled. The mind is the source of unwholesomeness and the body is a gathering of wrongdoings. Contemplate this and you will gradually turn away from the cycle of birth and death.

Second, realize that more desire causes more suffering. The weariness of the cycle of birth and death arises from greed and desire. Lessen desire and be without any wishes and the body and mind will be at ease.

Third, realize that the mind cannot be satisfied but only seeks more, increasing its wrongdoing and unwholesomeness. A bodhisattva is not like this; he is always satisfied with what he has, is peaceful in poverty, and upholds the Way. Wisdom is his only concern.

Fourth, realize that laziness leads to downfall. Be diligent and break through the evil of affliction. Defeat the four kinds of mara and escape the prison of the five aggregates and the three realms.

Fifth, realize that ignorance gives rise to the cycle of birth and death. A bodhisattva is always mindful, studies widely, listens more, increases his wisdom, and becomes more eloquent in order to teach all beings great joy.

Sixth, realize that those who are poor and suffering have more resentment, and that this leads them to create unwholesome conditions. A bodhisattva practices giving and has equal concern for friend and foe. He does not recollect past unwholesome deeds committed against him, nor does he hate unwholesome people.

Seventh, realize that wrongdoing comes from the five desires. Even though you are an ordinary person, do not be stained by worldly pleasures. Always be mindful of the triple robe, the bowl, and dharma instruments, and be willing to leave home, uphold the Way purely, practice the holy life well, and have compassion for all beings.

Eighth, realize that the cycle of birth and death is a raging fire and that suffering is boundless. Initiate the Mahayana mind to universally help all beings and vow to shoulder the boundless suffering of sentient beings so that all sentient beings may reach great joy.

These eight realizations are the realizations of all Buddhas and bodhisattvas. Diligently practice the Way and compassionately cultivate wisdom. Take the Great Dharma Vessel and reach the shore of nirvana, then return again to the cycle of birth and death to liberate sentient beings. Use these eight realizations to teach all beings and allow sentient beings to awaken to the suffering of the cycle of birth and death, turn away from the five desires, and cultivate the mind on the noble path. If a disciple of the Buddha recites these eight realizations in every thought he can eliminate boundless wrongdoings, progress towards bodhi, and quickly attain right enlightenment, forever cut off birth and death and always be happy.

Overview

The Eight Realizations of a Bodhisattva Sutra

Introduction

An Overview of the Sutra

A basic teaching of the Buddha is that all things are caused and that nothing comes into being without a reason. This way of thinking is so fundamental to Buddhism that all Buddhist sutras begin with an explanation of the causes that led to their inceptions. There is only one exception to this rule—the *Eight Realizations of a Bodhisattva Sutra*. This sutra does not have an introductory section that states where the sutra was spoken, to whom it was spoken, and who was responsible for remembering it. The introductory part of this sutra may have been omitted when it was translated into Chinese near the end of the second century of the common era.

The *Eight Realizations of a Bodhisattva Sutra* is one of the first Buddhist sutras ever translated into Chinese. It reads like a short summary of Mahayana Buddhism, and surely it was selected for early translation for precisely this reason. It is characterized by its brevity, clarity, and completeness. The *Eight Realizations of a Bodhisattva Sutra* is a mature compendium of the main ideas of

Mahayana Buddhism. Its early translation into Chinese was clearly an attempt to introduce Buddhism to an intelligent and receptive non-Buddhist Chinese audience. This sutra, along with the *Sutra in Forty-Two Sections,* which is the first sutra ever translated into Chinese, and which is also a brief work, prepared China for the vastly detailed Buddhist literature that was to pour into it over the next five centuries.

The eight realizations discussed in this sutra are also mentioned in the *Agama Sutras,* the *Sutra of Teachings Bequeathed by the Buddha,* and the *Satyasiddhi Sastra.* The original Sanskrit version of the sutra has been lost.

Tradition has it that the teaching contained in the *Eight Realizations of a Bodhisattva Sutra* was prompted by a question asked of the Buddha by one of his wisest disciples, Aniruddha. While the Buddha was staying at the Jeta Grove in Sravasti, Aniruddha is reported to have asked him the following question:

"Oh Buddha, those of us who are monks know that our behavior must be guided by the Six Points of Reverent Harmony, and that we must be selfless with each other. We also know that we must treat all other sentient beings with compassion and kindness. Oh Buddha, how are lay people to behave? And how are those of us who are monks to behave when we interact with lay people? Please tell us how they are to become enlightened and how they should behave if they want to achieve nirvana."

The Buddha replied, "Aniruddha, you have asked a good question. This question pertains to the realizations of all bodhisattvas. I will now explain to you that which, night and day, you should hold in your mind..."

The *Eight Realizations of a Bodhisattva Sutra* has been praised by Buddhist masters down through the centuries. Its greatness lies in its emphasis on the importance of life in this world. Though it is a short text, it is infinitely valuable for it shows how the Buddha intended his teachings to be used. This sutra is like a compass and navigational chart. It offers all of the wisdom we will ever need to steer our lives away from confusion and fear toward the peace and security of the shores of truth.

The Teacher and the Teaching

Sakyamuni Buddha, who is the speaker of this sutra, was born a prince in Kapilavastu in what is now Nepal. At the age of twenty-nine, he renounced all of his worldly privileges to pursue the truth. After six years of practice, he became enlightened one evening while meditating under a bodhi tree. For the next forty-five years, he taught others how to realize what he had seen. The giving and compassion that he displayed in teaching the Dharma for so many years form a living core around which all of the rest of Buddhism clusters. Though the teachings of the Buddha contain many philosophical ideas, they must never lead us into believing that they have no application to life or that we should turn our backs on others because of them. The compassionate example of Sakyamuni Buddha stands as a constant reminder that the well being of others is fully as important as our own.

The word *Buddha* means "enlightened one" or "awakened one." Sakyamuni Buddha is the Buddha of our realm. He is usually referred to as "the Buddha." There are many other Buddhas residing in many other realms in the universe. The Buddha taught that there are more Buddha realms in the universe than there are grains of sand in the Ganges River. Just as the night sky teems with stars, so the universe is teeming with life.

Sakyamuni Buddha did not invent the truths that he taught. He discovered them. He taught that all human beings can do what he did. He said that when a human being makes his consciousness perfectly pure, he will see the truth that underlies all things. In that moment he will become enlightened. As we delve more deeply into the *Eight Realizations of a Bodhisattva Sutra*, we will learn much more about the truths that the Buddha taught. His teachings are often described as a "path" because they lead us toward discovering the truth for ourselves. The truths of Buddhism are living truths and they cannot be handed to us by anyone. They must be discovered and experienced by each and every one of us. The purpose of the Dharma is to teach us how to see for ourselves.

The word *bodhisattva* is a compound of two Sanskrit words *bodhi* and *sattva*. *Bodhi*, which means "enlightened," is derived from the same word that gives us *Buddha*. *Sattva* means "sentient being." A sentient being is any being with consciousness or the potential to become conscious. Animals and insects are sentient beings, while plants are not. A bodhisattva is a person who dedicates his life to the enlightenment of all other sentient beings in the universe. Sometimes this word is translated as "enlightening being" because bodhisattvas are dedicated to the "enlightening" of all other sentient beings. Some bodhisattvas are exceptionally great beings who can manifest at will for the good of others. Other bodhisattvas are merely ordinary people who have made the extraordinary vow to dedicate themselves to the well being of others. The *Eight Realizations of a Bodhisattva Sutra* is directed mainly at ordinary bodhisattvas. It is intended to teach them how to behave in the world, and how to help others. It teaches that the life of a bodhisattva must be characterized by compassion, caring, wisdom, and kindness. In this sutra, as well as in many others, the Buddha explains that the bodhisattva path is an active path that leads into life and that it is not a passive way that seeks only to retreat from life.

Buddhism is an eminently practical religion because it teaches us how to live in this world. It is also the most mystical of religions because it shows us how to experience transcendental awareness in every moment of our lives. The Buddha is sometimes called the "great doctor" because he shows us how to cure ourselves of the ills of ignorance. He is sometimes called the "great teacher" because he teaches us how to free ourselves from the greed and anger that bind us to the world. He is sometimes called the "great ox" because he uses his strength to draw us toward the truth. In the *Eight Realizations of a a Bodhisattva Sutra*, the Buddha summarizes the principal points of his teaching. As its introductory verse says, this sutra ideally should be "recited with a sincere mind each morning and night."

The Translator and the Translation

All Buddhist sutras originally were talks given by the Buddha between the years of 428-383 BCE. They were remembered in a vibrant and complex oral tradition for hundreds of years before they were set down in writing. Though the Buddha spoke a language called Old Maghadi, his teachings were first recorded in the Sanskrit and Pali languages because these languages had well developed writing systems. A written record of a talk by the Buddha is generally known as a "sutra." The word *sutra*, from which we derive the English word "suture," means "stitched together." Very early Buddhist sutras were recorded on palm leaves and stitched together. Once they were written down, the sutras were carried to areas outside of the Buddhist world and translated into many other languages, including Central Asian languages, Chinese, Tibetan, Mongolian, and many others. Korea and Japan used Chinese versions of the sutras throughout most of their histories. Only a portion of the entire collection of Buddhist sutras has been translated into English. Buddhist literature is voluminous because of the large number of talks given by the Buddha, who taught for forty-five years. The spread of Buddhism through Asia generally followed established trade routes. After leaving the Ganges River valley, it spread north into Kashmir and Central Asia via the silk road. It began to enter China from the oasis states of Central Asia which lie to China's west. Buddhist sutras and teachers also entered China via sea routes from India.

The translator of the *Eight Realizations of a Bodhisattva Sutra* was a Parthian monk, whose name in Chinese is An Shigao. His Parthian name is unknown. He probably traveled through Central Asia to arrive in China in 148 CE. Since the Parthians were excellent sailors, it is also possible that he traveled to China by sea. Parthia was a large kingdom located to the south of the Caspian Sea in what is now Iran. An Shigao is reported to have been a Parthian prince who renounced royal life to enter a Buddhist monastery. He is said to have had superb linguistic abilities and was able to communicate with animals. He made his translations in Loyang, one of China's ancient capitals, and now the city of Xian. An Shigao is said to have known over thirty languages and translated over 100 sutras into Chinese, but only about thirty of them exist today. He is the most important early translator of Buddhist sutras into Chinese. In addition to the *Eight Realizations of a Bodhisattva Sutra*, he is known to have translated parts of the *Abdhidarma*, which contains the basic teachings of Buddhism.

He is the first person to teach Buddhist meditation techniques in China. Chinese records show that he left Loyang to travel south in 170 CE. It is not known what became of him after that.

For All Disciples of the Buddha

This sutra is different from all other Buddhist sutras because it does not begin with the line: "Thus have I heard, at one time, the Buddha was in such and such a place before a gathering of people..." As mentioned earlier, An Shigao may have decided that the sutra would be more accessible to his Chinese audience if he left its introductory passage out. The usual introduction to a Buddhist sutra always says who was present at the talk, what was said, when it was said, where it was said, and who remembered it.

The verse at the beginning of the sutra must stand as its introduction: "For all disciples of the Buddha, each morning and night, recite with a sincere mind, these eight realizations of a bodhisattva." This verse is clearly asking us to chant the sutra at least once every morning and night. Chanting a sutra is a common and very beneficial practice for it steadies the mind, brings peace to our homes, reminds us of the Dharma, and helps us focus our energies on things that matter. Chanting is an especially important part of Buddhism as it is practiced in China.

This verse is directed to "all disciples of the Buddha." A "disciple of the Buddha" is someone who has formally taken refuge in Buddhism and accepted Sakyamuni Buddha as his teacher. Others may respect Buddhism and learn from the teachings of the Buddha, but they are not truly disciples until they have actually taken refuge. Needless to say, this does not mean that non-Buddhists cannot learn from this, or any other, Buddhist sutra. Very few people would decide to become Buddhists without first understanding what the teachings mean.

    When a sutra is chanted, we must have the right attitude. Just as beautiful music cannot be played on an instrument that is out of tune, so we cannot receive the full benefit of chanting if our attitudes are confused, self-centered, suspicious, close-minded, or condescending. Before chanting we should settle our minds as if in meditation. We should then approach the words of the Buddha with the utmost sincerity. We should think of him as our good friend and teacher, as someone who wants to help us. Then with great concentration, we should chant the sutra. We may chant alone or in a group, and we may chant loudly or softly. In part we are actively speaking, and in part we are resting and going deeper into the meditative states on which all higher wisdom is founded. In times when we are not chanting, we should reflect on the meaning of the sutra and allow its import to reverberate in our minds and throughout our lives.

Chapter I

The First Realization

Realize that this world is impermanent and that nations are dangerous and fragile. The four great elements lead to suffering and are empty and the five aggregates are without a self. All things arise, cease, change, and become different; they are illusory, not real, and cannot be controlled. The mind is the source of unwholesomeness and the body is a gathering of wrongdoings. Contemplate this and you will gradually turn away from the cycle of birth and death.

Chapter One

The First Realization
The Nature of This World

The *Eight Realizations of a Bodhisattva Sutra* can be divided into two parts. The first part is the first realization, while the second part is the remaining seven. This first realization is concerned with the Buddha's analysis of this world; in this realization he discusses impermanence, emptiness, the nature of mind, and the cycle of birth and death. The purpose of this discussion is to make us understand the nature of the world that we live in. In the seven realizations that follow, the Buddha will teach us how to live in the world. The most important ideas in the first realization are impermanence and emptiness. I will discuss these ideas in greater detail below.

Impermanence

The sutra says, "Realize that this world is impermanent and that nations are dangerous and fragile." The Buddha's explanation of life in this world is founded on the idea of impermanence. He taught that everything changes and that nothing stays the same. The Buddha emphasized impermanence not to discourage us, but to make us realize the true nature of existence. If we understand that everything is impermanent, we will behave differently than if we mistakenly believe that this world is not subject to constant change.

The Buddha concludes the *Diamond Sutra* by saying, "All phenomena are like dreams, like illusions, like bubbles, like shadows. They are like dew, like lightning. And they should be contemplated as such." The images used in this very famous string of metaphors are images of impermanence. By saying that all phenomena are like dreams, bubbles, shadows, dew, or lightening, the Buddha is saying in a graphic way that all phenomena change, and that they change quickly. Dreams come and go, bubbles pop, dew evaporates in the sun, and lightening only flashes for a second. Nothing stays the same. All things change.

In the *Sutra of Great Wisdom* the Buddha says, "This world is impermanent. It is like the moon in the water. All that we do is torn asunder by the winds of change." Again, he is not trying to dishearten us with this statement. He is just telling us how it is. The moon in the water is beautiful, and we may enjoy it as long as it lasts, but no one should believe that it is permanent. We cause ourselves to suffer whenever we attempt to cling to the phenomena of this world, which by their very natures are evanescent. Everything is torn asunder by the winds of change.

There is an old story that well illustrates the importance of accepting change. Once during the time of the Buddha there was a wealthy woman whose only child died suddenly. The woman was so anguished by her son's death that she carried him in her arms into the street where she frantically asked anyone who would listen to her if they knew of some way to bring him back to life. People only looked at her with sadness as they shook their heads. At last she came upon someone who told her to go to see the Buddha. "Maybe he can help you," the person said. With that advice, the woman rushed to where the Buddha was staying and asked him if he could help her.

The Buddha said, "To save this child you will need four or five mustard seeds obtained from a family that has never known death."

The woman rushed back into the street and began going from house to house asking if she could have some mustard seeds. The seeds themselves were easy to obtain, but no one could say that their family had not known death. At last she gave up searching and went back to the Buddha. When she saw him again she noticed that he wore an expression of profound compassion. And with that she also understood that nothing is permanent and that everyone must die. At last she was ready to give up her impossible attachment to a child who already was gone.

People change, phenomena change, our thoughts, dreams, feelings, ideas, and lives change all the time. Nothing stays the same. The *Treatise on the Perfection of Great Wisdom* says that change occurs in two basic ways: from moment to moment, and over longer periods of "successive" or "continuous" change. Momentary change is apparent all around us. The wind blows, sounds come and go, our hearts beat, our eyes blink—everything in us and around us changes from moment to moment. Successive change is also apparent all around us, but some thought is required to see it. Successive change means a continuous accumulation of momentary changes in something that we normally think of as enduring over time, such as a nation, a geological formation, a sports team, a traditional way of doing something, a language. As the years go by, a vast number of momentary changes accumulate in such entities. Eventually, they will not even resemble their original states anymore. The erosion of sea coasts and the evolution of species on earth are also good examples of successive change. In the moment we do not notice these changes, but over time they appear very large. When the Buddha says in this realization that "nations are dangerous and fragile," he is referring to the idea of successive change.

The *Madhyanta-vibhaga-tika* says that change can be understood as being universal to all phenomena by understanding that no phenomenon stands alone. All phenomena depend on other phenomena, and thus when any one of them changes, all of them change.

Once we are convinced that all things change, there are two basic ways that we can use this information. We can use it to prepare ourselves to accept that which we must accept, and we can use it to inspire ourselves to look toward the future with a hopeful and positive attitude. Most people feel gloomy when they contemplate the truth of impermanence because they only imagine good things turning to bad. But just as good things can turn to bad, so also can bad things turn to good. Change leads us out of difficult situations, it relieves us of our cares, and it is the process by which we transform ourselves into Buddhas. If nothing changed, we would never grow.

The sutra says "All things arise, cease, change and become different; they are illusory, not real, and cannot be controlled." This means that if we believe that anything has a "stable essence" or that it is not subject to change, we are being distracted from the truth by an "illusory appearance." All things that arise must change.

The concept of change or impermanence is important in and of itself, but it is also important because the Buddha used this concept to explain an even deeper idea that is even more central to his teaching. If we can grasp what the Buddha meant by successive change in a nation or along a coast line, we should also be able to grasp that the book we are holding, the chair we are sitting on, and the clothes we are wearing are subject to successive change as well. We should be able to see that everything for which we have a word or a concept is subject to successive change. Though the things of our world may seem substantial, when we think about them deeply we can see that they are essentially evanescent and that they cannot really ever be grasped or held. All that we can hold onto is an illusory appearance that is fundamentally devoid of all absolute qualities.

In the *Diamond Sutra* the Buddha asserts that even our minds have no essence that can be obtained when he says, "The mind of the past cannot be obtained, the mind of the present cannot be obtained, and the mind of the future cannot be obtained." This succinct truth has the unique quality of being both self-evident and difficult to obtain!

The concept of impermanence goes hand in hand with the Buddha's teachings on emptiness. *Emptiness* means that nothing has a permanent "self-nature" or essence. Since everything changes all the time, nothing can be said to be any more substantial than the moon reflected in the water, or the dew on the morning grass, or the dream that just eluded us.

Emptiness

The second important idea in this first realization is the idea of emptiness. The Sutra says "the four great elements lead to suffering and are empty and the five aggregates are without a self; they arise, cease, change, and become different; they are illusory, not real, and cannot be controlled."

Emptiness is a special term in Buddhism. It means "having no permanent, definite, or absolute aspect whatsoever." The Buddha taught that everything within the phenomenal universe is *empty*. Nothing within it has any permanent, definite, or absolute aspect whatsoever. Nothing has any stable essence. If one wants to understand the teachings of the Buddha, it is as important to understand emptiness as it is to understand impermanence.

Buddhist thinkers sometimes say that there are six basic ways to understand emptiness. The first is to understand that our sense organs are empty. The second is to understand that everything our sense organs perceive is empty. The third is to understand that the interaction between our sense organs and what they perceive is empty. The fourth is to understand that the concept of emptiness itself is empty. The fifth is to understand that everything in the universe is empty. The sixth is to understand that there is no permanent aspect anywhere beyond the reaches of the universe, no matter how we may conceive of what the universe is.

None of this says that the world is not here, or that nothing exists, or that we must despair of our condition. Emptiness simply means that nothing has an unchanging essence or self-nature that is independent of other things. To believe otherwise is to be deluded.

The *Treatise on the Perfection of Great Wisdom* says, "Since phenomena arise due to extrinsic causes and conditions, they do not have a self-nature, and thus they are empty."

The *Ghana-vyuha Sutra* says, "Without emptiness, there is no form. Without form, there is no emptiness. The two are like the moon and the light of the moon: From first to last they are always together."

Emptiness is a far-reaching idea that has many profound consequences. When we understand emptiness, we change the way we live and the way we feel. When we do not understand emptiness, we tend to cling to things and form strong emotional reactions to what are really only illusory appearances. The concept of emptiness flies in the face of basic human psychology, for one of our strongest tendencies is to treat ourselves, other people, and the things of the world as if they were permanent, enduring entities that can and should be imbued with all of the significance our passion would like them to have. The Buddha reminds us *that all things arise, cease, change and become different; they are illusory, not real, and cannot be controlled.* Emptiness is both a philosophical term and a practical technique for overcoming the delusions of this world. The Buddha intended us to understand it in both ways.

While emptiness is a profound philosophical idea, it is also something that can be experienced. Direct perception of the emptiness and unity of all things is the theme of many Chan stories. Deep understanding of emptiness helps us maintain a sense of reverence for everything that happens to us. The following story took place in the nineteenth century.

Once, Master Yishan was getting ready to take a bath. Since the bath water was too hot, he asked a disciple to bring him a bucket of cold water. The disciple came with the cold water and added enough to bring the temperature of the bath down. Then he threw the remaining water on the ground.

Yishan said, "Why are you being so wasteful? Everything has value and everything should be appreciated for what it is. Instead of throwing that water away, you could have used it to water our plants. Even a single drop of water has infinite value if you truly understand how rare and wonderful it is, and how it is interconnected with all other things in the universe."

After hearing this, the disciple experienced a small awakening and decided to change his name to "Water Drop." Later in life, this disciple became the famous Japanese master, Master Tekisui (1822-1899), whose name means "Water Drop." Master Tekisui was respected by everyone who knew him.

Many years after the incident described above, Tekisui was teaching the Dharma when he was asked by one of his listeners, "What is the most precious thing in the universe?"

Tekisui replied, "A drop of water."

Then another listener asked him, "If emptiness subsumes all things in the universe, what subsumes emptiness?"

Tekisui replied simply, "A drop of water."

Master Tekisui understood that since the mind is one with all things, it is also one with a single drop of water, and the drop of water is one with all. When we truly understand emptiness, our minds are freed from the constraints of believing in an impossible essence or a rigid permanence among things. In this freedom they are able to soar to the highest heights, to expand beyond all limits, or to see the universe in a single drop of water. When emptiness is fully understood, our minds grow beyond the confinements that hold us fixed in a deluded assessment of the conditions of our lives. The teachings of the Buddha are at once practical, philosophical, and mystical, for to experience his teachings is to experience life as you never have before.

The Emptiness of the Four Great Elements

The four great elements, earth, water, fire and wind, are the four basic material components of the phenomenal universe. All things in the universe can be described in terms of the four great elements. When the Buddha says the four great elements cause suffering and are empty, he is saying that all material phenomena are without any stable essence and that to believe otherwise is to suffer. There is nothing that does not change and nothing that can be clung to. Everything is empty. When we mistakenly believe that we can discover absolutes within the four great elements, we will begin to create conditions that will lead to suffering for the simple reason that we are wrong.

A human body is comprised of earth, water, fire, and wind. Some parts of us are solid (earth), some are liquid (water), we must heat ourselves (fire), and we must breathe (wind). If any one of these parts were to become weak, we would become sick. If any one of these parts were suddenly to withdraw from us, we would die. Plants can also be understood in this way, for plants must grow in the earth, they must be watered, they must have sunshine, and they must have air. If any of these elements is missing, a plant will quickly die. In modern English when we say "the material world," we are essentially talking about the same thing that the Buddha was talking about in his discussions of the four elements. The four elements cause suffering when we fail to understand that they are both impermanent and empty. When we fail to understand the true nature of the world we live in, we suffer. When we cling to dreams or ideas that have no true essence or self-nature, we set ourselves up to feel disappointment and pain.

There is an old story that illustrates this point in an interesting way. Once in a very remote part of China, there lived an old couple who were quite well off. They had a lot of land, a big house, and plenty of money. The couple was not happy, though, because they had not been able to have children. They asked everyone they could why they were unable to have children, but no one in that region was able to tell them. Then one day a young Buddhist monk who had only recently entered the order visited their village. The old couple was delighted at his appearance, and they invited him to their house so they could offer him food and pay their respects to him. After he had eaten, they asked him to speak about the Dharma and explain to them why they were unable to have children. Since the monk was young and not knowledgeable about Buddhism, he was not sure how to answer them. As the couple waited expectantly, he became more and more nervous about what to say.

As his silence persisted, the old couple, who mistook his reticence for wisdom, proceeded to bow down before him. They touched their foreheads to the floor and waited for him to speak. The young monk, who had no idea what to say, began to feel very uncomfortable. In his anxiety, he began to think that it was a lot harder to be a monk than he had first realized. Here were two people imploring him to explain something he knew nothing about. In his consternation, he exclaimed, "This is really difficult!"

When the couple heard him say that, they breathed a sigh of relief for they understood him to be describing their situation, not his. It had been difficult! All those years they had tried to have children, but nothing had ever come of it. In gratitude, they raised and lowered their heads in a series of short bows before him.

When the monk saw the effect his words had on the couple, and that his attempt to find relief from his situation had only worsened it, he became so anxious he began to perspire. What was he to do? If he said nothing he would disappoint the couple, and yet if he said something he would only expose his own ignorance. Thinking simply of himself, he said, "Such suffering!"

When the old couple heard this, they again were relieved, for here was someone who really understood them! For years they had tried to have children, yet they had never met with success. Truly that was suffering! As they absorbed the fullness of his remarks, the old couple began to weep uncontrollably where they knelt on the floor. All those years, and now at last, someone who truly understood their plight! As the couple continued to weep, the young monk thought to himself that the situation was going from bad to worse. In a state of great anxiety, he quietly left the room.

The couple cried together for a long time. Then they waited quietly and reverently for the young monk to continue, but when they did not hear his voice for a long time, they at last raised their heads to see that he was gone.

"Wondrous!" they exclaimed, for they were so overwhelmed by their experience that they were sure the monk had been a living Buddha sent especially to them to explain the truth of suffering. "What a wonder!" they exclaimed as they absorbed the deep meaning of his profound message. And from that day on, they worried less about what they did not have and much more about what they could give to others. Their practice of the Dharma improved for their understanding of the nature of phenomenal existence at last was built upon the truth. And with this truth they found joy, for no longer did they invest all of their hopes in the evanescent world of phenomenal change.

The Buddha taught the truths of impermanence and emptiness not to harm us or make us sad, but to help us rid ourselves of the deluded thinking that binds us to things we cannot have, or cannot have for long. Understanding impermanence and emptiness can liberate us from much suffering and hardship, for these truths can help us look beyond the "illusory appearances" of things into the deep nature of life that alone is real.

The Emptiness of Self

After explaining that the four elements are empty, the Buddha adds that the five aggregates, form, feeling, perception, mental formation and consciousness, are without a self. This means that the self is empty. Just as all things, all ideas, all phenomena, and all phenomenal states are empty, so too are all people. Just as there is no "stable essence" within phenomena, so there is no "stable essence," or enduring "self" within people. The permanence and fulfillment that we all long for cannot be found in the body or in the self. The Buddha taught that true spiritual fulfillment can only be found after we have overcome these delusions. Though this truth may sound harsh to some, it is not harsh, for the panoramas that open before the mind after one accepts that the five aggregates are without a self is far more wondrous than anything that was seen before.

The *Great Commentary on the Five Aggregates* says, "Why did the Buddha teach the five aggregates? He taught them to help us cure three forms of delusion and all that follows from them. The three forms of delusion are: the delusion of having a self-nature, the delusion of having a self that perceives, and the delusion of having a self that acts."

The *Satyasiddhi Sastra* says, "The sense of self that arises with the five aggregates is based on the body and the belief that the body is real; in truth, there is no self within the aggregates and that is why they are called conditioned aggregates."

The five aggregates explanation is a behavioral/perceptual analysis of the workings of our everyday minds. The Buddha said that the workings of this mind are almost always deluded because people fall into the trap of believing that there is an agent or a self lurking within them, and that this agent or self is the ultimate beneficiary of all that the mind does. The five aggregates explanation of this mistaken notion about the mind is intended to deconstruct the foundation upon which this mistake rests. If we can see our minds for what they are, the Buddha said, we will know how to use them to help rather than harm the world we live in. When we do not understand them for what they are, we tend to become selfish and to be motivated by greed, anger, and ignorance. I will discuss each of the five aggregates in more detail below.

The sutra says, "the five aggregates are without a self." That represents the Buddhist viewpoint of non-self.

What are the five aggregates? They are form, feeling, perception, mental formation and consciousness, which combine to form a person. Form corresponds to what we would call the material, or physical, factors of experience while the other four aggregates are mental factors.

Form consists of the four great elements, the five sense organs (eye, ear, nose, tongue and body), and the sense objects (form, sound, smell, taste and touch). Form is also described as being that which "changes and obstructs" because all material objects are subject to change, are impermanent, and act as obstructions to our cultivation.

Feeling describes the sensation experienced when we com in contact with form, and they are of three kinds: pleasant, unpleasant, and indifferent. Any object that is experienced results in one of these three kinds of feelings.

Perception is the process by which we create an image in the mind through recognition or identification. Perception includes attachment to the external objects, recollecting the past, and assuming the future.

Mental formations can be described as a conditioned response to the object of experience. These responses have moral consequences in the form of wholesome, unwholesome, and neutral effects.

The aggregates of consciousness have the nature of discriminating the sense objects. The eyes come in contact with the visible objects and eye consciousness arises to distinguish which color is blue, yellow, white and black. The ears come in contact with sound and ear consciousness arises to distinguish what sounds are pleasant or unpleasant. The nose comes in contact with smell and smell consciousness arises to distinguish which smell is fragrant or odorous. The tongue comes in contact with taste and tongue consciousness arises to distinguish which taste is sour, sweet, bitter or spicy. The body comes in contact with objects and body consciousness arises to distinguish which is cold, warm, soft or hard.

One day the great Chan Master Huineng (638-713) visited Faxing Temple in Canton, China. In the courtyard of the temple he saw two monks arguing heatedly about something. Huineng drew closer and heard that they were arguing about a banner that was flying above the temple gate.

Huineng heard one monk say, "The wind is moving." The other monk replied, "The banner is moving."

Huineng, who had drawn close to the monks by this time, said, "The wind is not moving and the banner is not moving. Your minds are moving."

The *Treatise on the Perfection of Great Wisdom* says, "Sentient beings arise out of the five aggregates and the conditions that underlie them."

The *Gradual Discourses of the Buddha* says, "The aggregate of form is like foam, the aggregate of feeling is like a bubble, the aggregate of perception is like a wild horse, the aggregate of mental formation is like the trunk of a banana tree, and thus the aggregate of consciousness is like magic." The Buddha said that the aggregate of mental formation is like the trunk of a banana tree because the trunk of a banana tree is comprised of leaves curled together in the shape of a trunk. It looks substantial, but it is not. Like magic the aggregate of consciousness is "nothing more than an illusion" since it is entirely empty.

The *Sutra of the Victorious King* compares the aggregates to houses. We seem to inhabit them and draw comfort from them, but in truth their "shelter" is more like a prison than a home.

The *Treatise on the Perfection of Great Wisdom* compares the five aggregates to mara for it is the aggregates that heap suffering upon us and keep us confined to the painful cycle of birth, sickness, old age and death.

Seeing through the five aggregates is not a mere intellectual exercise. It is both a profound experience and one of the principal goals of all Buddhist practice. The following passage comes from the autobiography of one of China's most influential monks, Master Hanshan (1546-1623). In this passage he describes what he saw the first time the delusion of the five aggregates fell away. The scene takes place on Mount Wutai, which is located in north China:

"One day after finishing my meal, I suddenly entered a deep meditative state. In this state, I perceived neither my body nor my mind. All I could see were the five great lights of deep consciousness. The tranquility of this state was awesome, and the world appeared in it as if it were being reflected in a great mirror. The mountains, rivers, and plains were imbued with a brilliant lucidity that had awareness, and yet when I looked for my body or mind, I could not find them anywhere."

When we see beyond the five aggregates, the container self which confines the fullness of human consciousness is washed away and the world appears "as if reflected in a great mirror." The five great lights of deep consciousness are the profound forces that underlie the four great elements plus emptiness.

The Mind is the Source of Unwholesomeness

The Buddha often explained emptiness and impermanence by getting people to think about how phenomena arise, change, and decline. The process of arising, changing, and declining is a general form of the cycle of birth and death. Birth corresponds to arising while death corresponds to declining. The purpose of these explanations is to make us focus on the details of change, and thereby realize that nothing is permanent. When we completely understand that nothing is permanent and that nothing has a "stable essence," we will understand that all appearances to the contrary are but "illusory appearances." An illusory appearance is any phenomena that we mistakenly believe is not empty.

The *Lankavatara Sutra* says, "All things arise from the mind and all things are extinguished in the mind."

The *Sutra of Teachings Bequeathed by the Buddha* says, "If you can control your mind, you can do anything."

There is a wonderful Chan story that illustrates how the mind tends to create its own world by grasping at interpretations that are not warranted by the facts. One day Master Ikkyu was traveling with a young monk when the two of them came to a river. On the bank of the river was a young woman who was afraid to cross the waters which were quite swift and deep. Out of compassion for her, Ikkyu volunteered to carry her across. When they reached the other side, Ikkyu let the young woman down and continued on his journey as before. Nothing more happened that day, but a few months later, the young monk spoke up.

"Master," he said, "There is something that has been bothering me for a long time. Can you please help me to understand it?"

"What is it?" Ikkyu asked.

The young monk said, "Do you remember a few months ago when we crossed that river and you carried the woman on your back? I cannot understand why you did that. Haven't you always taught us to avoid contact with women?"

Ikkyu looked at the young monk and sighed. "Look at you," he said. "Do you see how your mind works? All I did was spend a few minutes carrying someone across a river, but you have been carrying her in your mind for months now!"

All things, both good and bad, start in the mind. Delusion is based in the workings of the mind. The sutra says "the mind is the source of unwholesomeness, and the body is a gathering of wrongdoings." The suspicions of the young monk in the story above were solely a product of his own mind. They were wholly disconnected from the true nature of Ikkyu's actions. Whenever we are suspicious, we live in a dark world of our own fears and wrongdoings.

The Buddha says that "the mind is the source of unwholesomeness" to make us realize that everything we have is of our own making. If we frequently engage in harmful or suspicious thoughts, our lives will become dark and unpleasant. If we frequently engage in beneficial and trusting thoughts, our lives will gradually become brighter and more joyful. Our minds are the turning points of our intentions and, thus, of our karma. There is no unwholesomeness "in the world." There is only unwholesomeness "in our minds." The *Avatamsaka Sutra* says, "The mind is a painter that paints many images."

The phrase "the body is a gathering of wrongdoings" echoes the point that all of illusory appearances are impermanent, changing and empty. They are described as *wrongdoings* because ultimately they have been created from bad intentions within our own minds. They are called a *gathering* because all delusion is made up of many parts. Delusion is delusion because we cannot clearly see its causes and conditions. The body appears because there is karma to generate it. There is karma because there is intention. There is a gathering of wrongdoings because our intentions circulate in a mind that seeks to justify itself on its own deluded terms. "The mind is the source of unwholesomeness" and thus the forms it sees are a "gathering of (its own) wrongdoings."

In the story above, the young monk was given to suspicion and low thoughts about the relationship between men and women and therefore he burdened himself for three months. The story below illustrates this same point in another way. Interestingly, this story also involves a river. Once there was a man walking along the bank of a river. As he walked, he watched a boatman push his boat into the water to prepare to take some people across the river. Just then a Chan master happened on the scene. The man stepped forward and said, "Master, I just watched that boatman push his boat into the water. When he did that he must have killed some of the crayfish and mussels that live at the water's edge. Who is to blame for their deaths? Is the boatman at fault or are his passengers to blame?"

The Chan master answered, "It is neither the boatman's fault nor the passengers' fault."

Confused by this answer, the man asked, "If it is not their fault, then whose fault is it?"

The Chan master replied, "It is your fault."

The Four Contemplations

The first realization of the *Eight Realizations of a Bodhisatttva Sutra* is concerned with what is generally called the Buddha's view of this world. This first realization is a description of the basic features of the world we live in. The points made in this realization are made in many other Buddhist sutras. The Buddha emphasized these basic points on many different occasions because it is essential that we have a correct understanding of the conditions of our lives if we are to know how to apply the rest of the Buddha's teachings. Buddhism is a religion of mental clarity. Its practices are based on reason. The central purpose of all Buddhist practice is the attainment of wisdom, or understanding. The Buddha frequently exhorted his followers to think for themselves. All of his teachings were designed to help us help ourselves. The last line of the first realization says "contemplate this and you will gradually turn away from the cycle of birth and death." Contemplation is central to all of the Buddha's teachings because mental clarity cannot be achieved without it. The first realization of this sutra contains four of the most important contemplations taught by the Buddha. These contemplations are meant to be used to help us overcome our problems. They should be applied to the actual events of our lives. Before we discuss them in detail, I will briefly say a few words about what the Buddha meant by the cycle of birth and death.

The cycle of birth and death has no beginning and no end. It is a cycle driven by karma and the impure intentions that underlie it. No sooner does one life end than another begins. No sooner does one karmic result wane than another waxes. The Buddha taught that we can liberate ourselves from the cycle of birth and death. He taught the importance of intention, and cause and effect to help us to turn away from the cycle of birth and death. When we understand what it is that causes us to be trapped in the cycle of birth and death, we will also understand how to free ourselves from it. The cycle of birth and death is maintained by wrong views and attachment to those views.

The Buddha taught us to free ourselves from it through right understanding. His teachings show us how to free ourselves from the passions of greed, anger, and ignorance that bind us to false notions of self, and to the "false appearance" of its importance. The contemplations mentioned in this first realization are meant to help us fully comprehend the world we live in and the parts that we play in that world. The right way to do the following contemplations is to think about them and apply them to your own life. These contemplations are not meant to be abstract ideals with little connection to our lives, but rather a basis for understanding the fullness of life as we actually live it in this world. As soon as these contemplations lead you to understand how one of their truths may be applied to your life, the right thing to do is apply it immediately. You will reap the benefits of your introspection very quickly. All anyone needs to do to be convinced of the truth of the Dharma is apply it to the life they are living. It always works.

The *Lotus Sutra* says, "The Dharma is so high, it can be difficult for people to understand. However, if we contemplate our own minds, it is easy to understand, for the mind, the Buddha, and sentient beings are all fundamentally one and the same."

The first contemplation mentioned in this sutra is the contemplation on impermanence. This contemplation is indicated by the line "this world is impermanent... nations are dangerous and fragile." In this contemplation, we reflect on the impermanence of all things, including ourselves. This contemplation has four main purposes: to make us understand the true nature of life in this world; to alert us to the dangers of clinging to phenomenal joys; to make us feel grateful for whatever we have; and to make us want to understand more about who and what we really are. Properly practiced, this contemplation should awaken within us a longing for higher states of awareness. The *Sutra of Vast Meaning* says, "The contemplation on impermanence helps us overcome sloth and laziness." The *Sutra of the Elder Sumagadha* says, "Contemplate that all things are impermanent and that nothing belongs to you... Understand that all things that come together must also come apart."

The second contemplation is the contemplation on emptiness. This contemplation is indicated by the line "the four great elements lead to suffering and are empty." This contemplation makes us aware that all things are produced from many other things and therefore, no one thing can be clung to. The four elements cause suffering only when we do not realize that they are empty. Once we fully understand that they are empty, they will not make us suffer any more. This contemplation has two basic purposes: to make us realize the true nature of all phenomena, including the phenomena of our own illusory self, and to help us overcome the difficulties of life, for when we understand the inherent emptiness of our problems, we are better equipped to see through them and not react with passionate or violent emotions. The *Pravara-devaraja-pariprecha Sutra* says, "Profound contemplation on emptiness takes us far from any individual point of view while it suffuses us with equanimity." The *Sutra on the Practice of Great Wisdom* says, "When we do the contemplation on emptiness, we should do it with our whole mind and not become distracted by anything, for if we are not distracted by anything then our realization will not be tainted with falseness."

The third contemplation is the contemplation on the absence of a true essence, or the absence of a true self. This contemplation is indicated by the line "the five aggregates are without a self." This contemplation is roughly the same as the contemplation on emptiness, though it is directed more at the illusory self of the person than at the phenomena that the person perceives. This contemplation, as does the contemplation on emptiness, recalls the line "all things arise, cease, change and become different. They are illusory, not real, and cannot be controlled." The *Sutra on the Emptiness of the Five Aggregates* says, "Contemplate the five aggregates and see that there is neither a self within them nor anything that might belong to a self. Then continue contemplating this and realize that in the entire world, there is nothing that you can really grasp or have.

The fourth contemplation is the contemplation on uncleanness. This contemplation is indicated by the line "the mind is the source of unwholesomeness and the body is a gathering of wrongdoings."

People always want others to have a wholesome mind but there are still many people who do not. There are those who commit sexual misconduct, steal from or rob others of their money or belongings, and speak unwholesome words. Although these wrongdoings are done by the body, hands and mouth, they are created in the mind.

Buddhism does not disapprove of wholesome love between a man and a woman but it does disapprove of love that is unhealthy and unsound. It is unfortunate when love becomes heartbreak and some people who once loved now assault or even kill others in the name of love.

Our bright inherent nature is covered if the mind is selfish. When the mind is too selfish, one will not consider justice, reason or friendship and is likely to do others harm.

A beautiful body is beloved by most of us and we desire the wealth of this world. However, at the end of our life, neither body nor wealth can follow us; only the mind, about which we have been less concerned, will follow us from this world to the next.

Nowadays, many people are busy with enjoyment of the body, and few are working to cultivate and purify their minds. No wonder there are so many imperfections in the world. Our bodies and our wealth do not truly belong to us. Only cultivating the mind can bring lasting happiness.

The mind easily leads us to commit wrongdoings, and causes us to have bodies. But, if we change the unwholesome to the wholesome, even though we still have bodies, they will be pure and clean.

If the four contemplations mentioned above are used often and applied to our lives, the day will come when we will stop making ourselves victims of our own self-defeating thoughts and behaviors. In the clarity that results from the absence of our customary confusion, we will see that our minds are far more wonderful than we had ever imagined before.

The First Realization

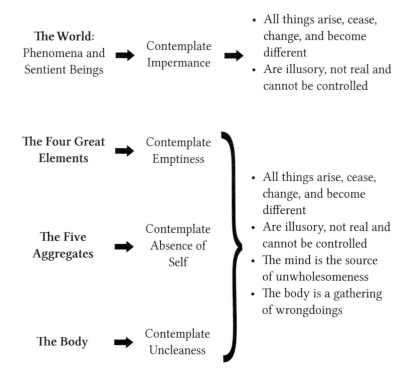

Chapter II
The Second Realization

Realize that more desire causes more suffering. The weariness of the cycle of birth and death arises from greed and desire. Lessen desire and be without any wishes and the body and mind will be at ease.

Chapter Two

The Second Realization
Greed is the Cause of Suffering

The first realization of this sutra concerns the Buddha's teachings on the nature of this world. The next seven realizations are concerned with his teachings on the nature of the human mind and how to live in this world. If we understand the principles discussed in the first realization, we will be in a very good position to understand how to apply the teachings of the next seven realizations to our lives.

Though the worlds that we see are fundamentally a product of our own minds, they usually do not appear this way to us. Like images in an intense dream, our perceptions appear to be wholly real to us, and not to have been generated by our own mental activity. For this reason, the Buddha taught many ways to help us comprehend the true nature of life. He taught that we are where we are not by accident or by any act of a supreme intelligence, but only by our own actions. Buddhism can seem difficult because it places so much responsibility on the individual practitioner. But ask yourself: Can anyone else understand for me? Can anyone else behave for me? Why should I not be responsible for my actions?

In this realization, the Buddha discusses desire, or greed. He says "Realize that more desire causes more suffering." Healthy desires include reasonable hunger, a balanced pursuit of shelter and clothing, reasonable social activity, and a balanced pursuit of hobbies or other amusements. When we have more desire we go beyond these parameters. Sometimes it takes wisdom to know when we are going too far in one direction or another, but for the most part, most of us know where our limits are. When we exceed them, we cause suffering. Desire strains our health, impairs our concentration, and often causes us to become angry or envious. Desire seduces us into lying both to ourselves and to our friends.

The Buddha taught that desire is a principal cause of our attachment to the illusory appearances of this world. Coupled with anger and ignorance, desire binds us to the cycle of birth and death, and to the recurring illusions that keep that cycle going. In modern times, there are literally thousands of ways that we can indulge our desires. And yet, who among us has never realized that desire leads to pain? Our cravings issue from a level that is far deeper than anything that can be satisfied by sensual gratification. Our deepest longings are an intimation of a truth that transcends all illusory appearances and all sensory needs. The Buddha taught that the way to find this truth is to understand that the illusory self is an illusion and that it maintains itself through greed and anger. *Pure Contemplation of the Dharma* says, "Greed is like a wolf, while anger is like an evil dragon."

When we give ourselves over to our desires, they quickly destroy us. When we moderate them, they gradually lead us to the center of our lives. Lying dormant in the storehouse of our deep

Buddha mind is the realization that we already are complete, and need not seek anything. The Buddha taught the Dharma to help us awaken this dormant realization.

There is a story in one of the sutras that illustrates the persistence of habitual desires, even when we have no need for them. Once there was a group of young women returning to their village from a fishing trip along the Ganges River. They carried baskets filled with fish on their backs. On their way home, the evening sky clouded over and the women were forced to seek shelter. Fortunately, a keeper of a flower shop saw them and invited them to stay in his place for the night. His shop was filled with fresh flowers. The women lay down to rest. Though they were all tired from their long day of walking and working along the river bank, not one of them could fall asleep. They were so unaccustomed to the fragrance of the flowers that they could not relax. At last one of them got up and went outside for her basket of fish. She brought it in and placed it in the middle of the room. With the odor of flowers covered by that of dead fish, the women soon fell asleep.

Desire is like the odor of dead fish. We get so used to it that when the pure fragrance of fresh flowers is offered us, we cannot relax. How tragic to remain bound by a habit generated by an illusion! Su Dongpo once wrote, "Human desires are inexhaustible, and yet that which can fulfill them is limited." The way to overcome desire is to understand what causes it. When the cause is understood, the cure is much easier to see.

Desires spring from harmful attachments, which are called *kleshas* in Sanskrit. Sometimes *kleshas* are also called "unwholesome mental functions," "defilements," "impurities," "obstacles," "deceptions," or "karmic attachments." Harmful attachments are selfish emotional or mental attachments that spring from greed, anger, or ignorance, and which cause us to harm other sentient beings. They seduce us into treating others with contempt in a vain attempt to raise ourselves above them, or to gratify ourselves at their expense. Nothing good ever comes of giving in to a harmful attachment.

The *Questions of Sakura Sutra* says, "Because there is love and hate, therefore there are harmful attachments... attachments of love and hate arise from our positive and negative feelings toward things." The *Sutra on Comprehending Great Wisdom* says, "The way to end harmful attachments is to be diligent and learn to base your actions on right thought." The *Sutra of Supreme Mindfulness* says, "Harmful attachments, though heaped like mountains, can be torn down by quiet introspection." The *Avatamsaka Sutra* says, "All sentient beings are possessed of innumerable harmful attachments." The *Sutra of Great Treasures* says, "Harmful attachments are like wild beasts for they act only in their own interests and won't be controlled." The *Treatise on the Perfection of Great Wisdom* says, "Wisdom is like a good arrow for it slays harmful attachments."

Harmful attachments can be anything from conscious desires to unconscious urges that we are not even aware of ourselves. When we are conscious of our attachments, they are generally easier to control than when we are not conscious of them. When we are not conscious of them, they are like seeds that lie within the soil of our being. When conditions are right, they grow into the tangled vines of desire. When conditions are not right, they lie dormant, often giving no sign of their presence. Harmful attachments can also be compared to rooms within the unconscious mind. When conditions are right, the doors to these rooms open and the urges behind them come forth. When conditions are not right, the doors remain closed, often giving us no indication of what lies inside. No one can escape these truths. Our minds are filled with a complexity of desire and passion that requires great effort to comprehend, let alone to control and overcome. Desire can be controlled by honest introspection and honest application of the truths revealed thereby. It cannot be controlled by indulgence because indulgence always plants more seeds of the same type.

There is an old story that illustrates the destructiveness of unbridled greed with convincing directness. Once there were two men named Chang and Wang, who were good friends. One day the two decided to take a walk together. On their way, they found a large piece of gold. Since they both had seen it at the same time, they decided to divide the piece of gold evenly between them.

Then Chang said to Wang, "The god of our city must have left this gold for us to find. Before we divide it, we should make an offering at the temple to show our gratitude."

Wang replied, "You are right. Why don't you go buy some food for our offering while I go to the temple to prepare things there?"

Both men felt very happy, and mara began stirring in their minds. As he walked to the market, Chang thought to himself: if Wang gets half of this gold, there will be less for me! As he walked to the temple, Wang thought to himself: if I had all of the gold for myself it would last much longer!

From these initial thoughts, terrible events were to follow, for the mind determines everything. Chang purchased a vial of poison with the food, while Wang concealed an axe near the table where they would eventually dine. Each of them thought that his well being was more important than the life of the other.

After they had completed their offering, as was the custom in their town, they took the food out back to eat it. As Chang emptied his vial of poison into the soup, Wang's axe fell on his head. With Chang safely dead, Wang decided that he might as well enjoy some soup before he left with the gold. Before he had consumed half of it, his abdomen was shot through with mortal pain. He died in the dirt beside the body of his former friend.

From the moment they formed the thought to kill one another both men planted the seeds of their own demises. Their retribution was especially swift and fitting. Had they controlled their greed, they could have lived for many years and enjoyed their good fortune. As it was, they lost everything. Happiness and prosperity can be safely based only on honesty and compassion. When greed enters the mix, the very same things that were a cause for joy quickly become a cause for sadness. The *Sutra of the All-Seeing Buddha Eye* says, "The cycle of birth and death is like rushing river rapids, or like waves in the sea." When we give into base desires, we are pulled into swift currents over which we have very little control. The *Commentary on the Sutra of Golden Light* says, "Greed is like an ocean current that flows without ceasing."

Harmful attachments are often described in Buddhist literature as impediments or hindrances because they block our view of the truth and prevent us from seeing our own Buddha nature. Sometimes, too, they are described as "deceptions" because they mislead us so easily. When they are described as deceptions, they are usually divided into two basic groups—deceptions of outlook and deceptions of thought or personality. Deceptions of outlook are our philosophies of life. They are wrong views. Wrong views quickly lead to wrong thoughts and wrong actions. They are the ultimate source of many secondary harmful attachments. Wrong views are basically those views which contradict the teachings of the Buddha. Deceptions of thought or personality are the internalized illusory appearances of the false self. They are nothing more than a vast collection of selected memories, self-serving excuses, self-centered fantasies, base intentions, and often violent defense mechanisms. They are what we draw on for most of our worldly behavior. Of course, the human character also contains intimations of enlightenment, love, kindness, joy, and all of the many promptings that lead us toward Buddhahood. The purpose of Buddhist practice is to use this second group of traits to overcome the first group.

The *Sutra in Forty-Two Sections* says, "When people give in to their desires, they become enchanted with excess and showing off. They become like a stick of incense that burns itself out—though others may admire its fragrance, the incense itself pays for the spell it casts by destroying itself."

As we examine the roots of our desires, we should consider them in the light of one or more of the contemplations mentioned at the end of chapter two. These basic contemplations were designed by the Buddha for no other purpose than to help us come to grips with the actual contents of our minds. Properly used, they will save us from much trouble and sadness. When we contemplate the inherent uncleanness of our desires, we will be less likely to be entranced by them. When we contemplate their essential emptiness, we will be less likely to be gulled by their vacuous insistence. When we contemplate the impermanence of both our desires and the conditions that gave rise to them, we will be more inclined to look inward for satisfaction, and not outward.

The *Treatise on the Middle Way* says, "When we are wholly selfless, harmful attachments do not arise." The *Sutra of Teachings Bequeathed by the Buddha* says, "People who are afflicted with many desires, always think about themselves and thus they have many troubles and cares. Though they may be wealthy, people who have many desires are poor in spirit. Though they may be poor, people who have few desires are rich in spirit."

Be Content in Body and Mind

Increased desire is cured by its own opposite: lessening desire. The sutra says "Lessen desire and be without any wishes and the body and mind will be at ease." When our desires are balanced and reasonable, we can be content. The Buddha taught that deep wisdom can be found only by following a "middle way" between dualistic extremes. The middle way can always be found by contemplating which side of a dualistic pair is contending for our attention. If we discover that we are becoming attached to money, we can find a healthy balance again by practicing giving, and reflecting on the fact that money is valuable only when it helps people, never when it harms them. If we find ourselves becoming attached to something that makes us angry or resentful, we can find a healthy balance by emphasizing compassion.

When we have less desires we will be happier because our lives will be easier to manage and we will have more time to consider that which is most important. Honest introspection always leads to the truth. If our introspection leads us to discover many harmful attachments within us, then we must take steps to understand their origins, as we look for ways to balance their deleterious influences. If it leads us to discover inklings of the enlightened Buddha mind within us, then we must encourage these inklings and cause them to grow and become more frequent. There is no better way to counteract the imbalances of samsara than to bathe them in the enlightened wisdom of the Buddha that already lies within us.

Contentment cures greed, compassion cures anger, and wisdom cures the confusion of many desires arising. When we know how to be satisfied with what we have, we can be happy anywhere and we will always be able to avoid increasing our desire and the terrible passions it releases. The *Surangama Sutra* says, "Wise contentment defeats the maras of the mind." The *Commentary on the Lotus Sutra* says, "Truth is like the sky, meditation like a great cloud, wisdom like the rain." Like the rain because it washes us and cleans us of our harmful desires. The *Sutra of Supreme Mindfulness* says, "Have few desires, be content, and put to rest all harmful clinging. Free yourself from your attachments, for when you taste greed you are like a fish that swallows a hook."

The following story reminds us that the Buddha can help us only if we are deeply receptive and willing to help ourselves. Once there was a man who was walking on a mountain road. As the dusty miles passed, he became tired and inattentive, and consequently lost his footing and fell down a steep precipice. As he fell, he managed to reach out and grab hold of a tree branch growing out of the cliff. Clutching the branch for dear life, he looked up and down. Far below him were the hard rocks at the bottom of the cliff, while above him there was only the sheer face of the cliff. As far as he could tell there was no way he could save himself. Then he saw the Buddha standing on the road above him. The Buddha was gazing on him with a look of great concern.

The man called out, "Oh Buddha, save me! Save me!"

The Buddha replied, "I will save you, but you must do as I say."

The man cried, "Anything, anything! I will do anything you say!"

"Let go of the branch," the Buddha said.

The man looked down at the rocks at the bottom of the cliff and thought that if he let go of the branch he would surely fall and be killed. His fears made him grab the branch more tightly.

When the Buddha saw that he was not going to let go, he said, "How can I save you if you don't let go?" And with that he turned and left.

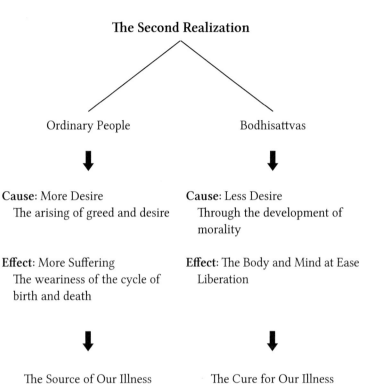

Chapter III

The Third Realization

Realize that the mind cannot be satisfied but only seeks more, increasing its wrongdoing and unwholesomeness. A bodhisattva is not like this; he is always satisfied with what he has, is peaceful in poverty, and upholds the Way. Wisdom is his only concern.

Chapter Three

The Third Realization
Contentment is the Source of Happiness

The second realization says that more desire leads to more suffering. The third realization says that knowing how to be satisfied with what we have is the cure for that suffering. In this realization, the Buddha explains that contentment is not simply an end in itself, but also a means to an even greater end, for when we are content with what we have and "peaceful in poverty," we will always be able to "uphold the Way." Contentment allows us to make "wisdom our only concern." If we are impatient and dissatisfied with our lives, we will be given to angry moods and to pursuits that waste our energies and only make our conditions worse.

This realization applies to all of us, for all of us are "poor" in one way or another. The true definition of a "poor person" is anyone who is so discontented with his circumstances that he has no time to become wise. "Poverty of contentment" is caused most of all by lack of honest introspection. Our minds cannot be satisfied, as the sutra says, because we do not stop long enough to think about what we are doing. As soon as we have what we once wanted, most of us just want more.

Greed begins in the mind, but it can quickly grow into a monster whose actions ruin many good things. There are seven major problems that arise from having strong desires: They may lead us to steal from others. They may lead us to borrow things and not return them. They may lead us to misappropriate wealth that has been entrusted to us. They may lead us to cheat our business partners through false reporting or through sly methods that lead to our having more control than was originally agreed upon. Strong desires may lead us to misuse company funds, materials, or office supplies. They may lead us to commit acts of extortion or blackmail. Strong desires may lead us to make money by owning or operating enterprises that encourage gambling, the irresponsible use of alcohol or drugs, prostitution, or the killing of animals. The Buddha said that these sorts of professions should be avoided whenever possible.

If we do not know how to be "satisfied with what we have" and "peaceful in poverty," our desires will multiply and grow for many lifetimes. One of China's great Buddhist masters, Master Daoan (312-385), once was given a huge amount of rice by a well meaning devotee who wanted to help him feed his disciples. The man gave so much rice, however, that Master Daoan hardly had enough room to store it all. When the rice at last had been put away, the master wrote a letter to the man. In it he said, "Thank you very much for the rice you gave us, but I must tell you that your gift has also caused us a lot of trouble because we have no place to put so much!"

Master Daoan understood that having too much can be as big a burden as having too little. He understood that seeking too many things in the world often creates more problems than it solves. When we are in the grip of excessive desire, we focus all of our energy on the sensory world outside of us. As long as that world has arranged itself around us in a way that we like, we will feel happy. The moment things go wrong, however, we will feel sad because we have not developed the inner strength and wisdom to know how to deal with life as it really is. Having excessive desires is part of an early stage in the life process. In this stage, we see ourselves as being at the center of everything. Since we believe that we are all important, our main interest in life is simply to gratify the needs of our "self." At a later stage of development, we will begin to see that the needs and feelings of others are also important and that the exclusive pursuit of our own desires leads only to suffering. We will begin to understand that desire does not really "gratify" us, but that it actually imprisons us within the walls of an illusion. At a still later stage, we will see that the entire notion of having a separate self is nothing more than a complex collection of "illusory appearances."

Once there was a man riding a mule. When he noticed that there was a man in front of him riding a horse, he began to feel inadequate and jealous. Then he looked behind him and saw another man pushing a cart. When he noticed how hard the man behind him was working and how much he was sweating, he began to feel better about himself and his mule. He said to himself:

> You ride on a horse, while
> I ride on a donkey.
> Looks like you're better off than me!
> Turning around,
> I see a man pushing his cart.

> Some are better off than me,
> Others are less fortunate than me.

There is a good lesson in this story. If we spend time comparing our lives to those who are "better" than us, we will make ourselves feel jealous and inadequate. If we spend time thinking about those whose circumstances are more difficult than our own, we will inspire ourselves to become sympathetic and compassionate. The Buddha taught that there are five basic ways in which wealth can be lost. It is good to contemplate these five ways because they help us understand that even the most grandiose of circumstances are impermanent. He said that wealth can be taken or destroyed by corrupt government officials, by natural disasters, by criminals, by war, or by wasteful family members. When we have wealth, we should use it to help others. When we share with those who are less fortunate than we are, we help them as we teach ourselves the value of giving. Wealth that is hoarded away is never really ours anyway. Wealth is really only a significant part of our lives when we use it.

Many years ago in China there was a king who wanted to study under a wise man. The king said to him, "If you accept me as your disciple and come live in my palace, you will always have the best food and clothing. And wherever you go you will ride in a carriage and you will always be accompanied by beautiful women."

The wise man replied that he preferred his life as it was. He said, "When I eat, I eat slowly and thus all of my food tastes good. When I walk, I pay attention to what is around me, and this is every bit as good as riding in a carriage. When I do things, I always think carefully before I act and I don't let myself be carried away by strong feelings, and this is better than the company of even the most beautiful of women."

It is not necessary to be poor to be a good Buddhist. The main point of this story, and others like it, is that we should learn to be satisfied with what we have. The Buddha did not teach us to despise wealth or to avoid money. He only taught that wealth should be used for the betterment of the world. When wealth is used for the good of society, it brings pleasure to everyone.

Growth can never be hurried. Words can only serve as aids to our improvement, never as substitutes for life itself. The Buddha taught the Dharma to help us learn the truth for ourselves. When he advises us to "be satisfied with what we have," he is not issuing a command or lecturing us. He is sharing insights gleaned from lifetimes spent in the pursuit of wisdom. Being satisfied with what we have allows us to stop and think, for when we are satisfied, we have time for introspection, and we have time to apply the conclusions of our introspection. The Dharma is designed to help us stop self-defeating behavior. When we make "wisdom our only concern," we begin leading our minds back to their original states of purity and wise innocence. The *Avatamsaka Sutra* says, "The Dharma is like a great sea. It is entered by faith and crossed by wisdom."

The *Treatise on the Perfection of Great Wisdom* says that great wisdom "is like the rising sun for it dispels mist and fog. The majesty of great wisdom affects people in two ways—ignorant people are frightened by it, while the wise are delighted... Wisdom does not come from anywhere and it does not go anywhere. The wise know that it cannot be sought among things." The treatise also says that great wisdom is "like vast space, without stain or defilement, without foolishness, or language. When we perceive wisdom in this way, we see the Buddha himself... The reason that Buddhas and bodhisattvas are able to help sentient beings is because their behavior arises out of wisdom."

The Third Realization

Ordinary People	Bodhisattvas
• The mind is unsatisfied • Always seeking more	• Satisfied with what he has • Peaceful in poverty, upholds the Way
Increased wrongdoing and unwholesomeness	Wisdom is his only concern

Chapter IV

The Fourth Realization

Realize that laziness leads to downfall. Be diligent and break through the evil of the affliction. Defeat the four kinds of mara and escape the prison of the five aggregates and the three realms.

Chapter Four

The Fourth Realization
Laziness Leads to Downfall

To be lazy is to not do what we know we should do. It is to waste time among sensory pleasures when we know that we should be emphasizing the development of our minds. The way to overcome negative tendencies is to stress their positive opposites. The way to overcome laziness is to be diligent. The Chinese philosopher Sunzi said that in life we are like swimmers in a river that is always flowing against our best interests. If we want to make progress, he said, we must swim against the current, for if we do not, we will be carried downstream. Indeed, just to stay in one place takes effort. The Buddha did not stay still and do nothing. He did not wallow in life's suffering or allow himself to be defeated by the enormity of the world's problems. He taught the Dharma instead. He saw the problem, figured out the solution, and then spent the rest of his life teaching it to others. Ksitigarbha Bodhisattva has vowed to remain in hell until all sentient beings have been liberated from it. The energy that lies behind this great vow is based on his knowledge of the positive fulfillment that lies at the end of suffering. Avalokitesvara Bodhisattva has vowed to go to any sentient being who is in need and who calls upon him. When great beings like these vow to give so much for the good of others, how can the rest of us not vow at least to save ourselves by our own efforts?

Laziness leads to downfall because it is based on ignorance and self-defeating behavior. When we emphasize those things that are negative or frightening in life, we tend to withdraw from the world and to dislike everything that happens to us. When we emphasize those things that are positive in life, we tend to reach out to others and to find pleasure in doing what we know we must do. Negative or lazy ways of thinking tend to be self-fulfilling prophesies. Discouraging thoughts tend to create discouraging outcomes because the conditions that prevail within our minds eventually become manifest in the events of our lives.

There was a time when the Buddha sent two monks to talk to people who had become seriously ill. One of the monks was old, while the other was a young man. Before long, people began to notice that when the older monk spoke to the ill they would quickly recover from their diseases, but when the younger monk spoke to them their conditions would only grow worse. The difference lay in what they were saying. The older monk always would say, "Everything is impermanent and so is your disease. If you continue to practice diligently, you will quickly get better." In contrast, the younger monk always said, "Illness is the result of bad karma. There is nothing you can do but accept these conditions and wait for them to pass." The older monk, who had lived longer, had a much deeper understanding of the Buddha's teachings than the younger monk. He knew that once we allow ourselves to feel defeated, our lives can only decline even more.

Diligence is that which helps us "break through the evil of afflictions." It is based on a deep resolution to become a better person, and not a superficial infatuation with mere concepts of goodness or piety. If we are to delve deeply into our minds, we must be prepared to deal with aspects of ourselves that are less than perfect. If we mistakenly equate diligence with an image of someone else's pious behavior, we will very likely fail to make the deep adjustments that our lives actually require. "The evil of afflictions" cause serious problems. Their hold on us is hard to break because these sorts of tendencies are very difficult for most people to recognize. Rather than confront the truth about ourselves, most of us prefer to explain away our behavior or to justify it in a way that makes us feel good but that does not get to the root of the problem.

Paramartha (499-569), who was one of the great early translators of Buddhist texts into Chinese, lived in China during very turbulent times. Paramartha was from northern India. He traveled to southern China in 546 to spread the Dharma. Though he worked in a strange land where he was constantly driven from one place to another by the battles that raged everywhere, he was able to keep his mind on his task. In the face of much human violence and cruelty, Paramartha succeeded in producing some of the gentlest and most beautiful translations of Buddhist literature ever done in Chinese. His translation of the *Treatise on Awakening of Faith in Mahayana* is a magnificent example of the triumph of spirit over adversity, for not only is this work an accurate and useful translation, it is also a beautiful one.

Paramartha succeeded where few before him had because he remained constant in his purpose and did not allow worldly trials to defeat him. How many of us could survive such hardships, let alone produce a great translation in the midst of them? Though he is remembered for the work he did while in China, Paramartha's most arduous work surely was done before he went to China. During his years in India he must have spent long periods of time in deep and honest introspection, for where else could he have discovered the inner resources that allowed him to be at once so sensitive and strong, so determined and receptive?

While we can learn much from the examples of others, examples alone will never suffice to make us diligent. The hard work of honest introspection and change is something that each of us must do for ourselves. The secret of really gaining something from Paramartha's life story lies in realizing what it was that made him able to do so much.

Buddhist sutras generally say that we gain ten benefits by practicing diligence: 1) we are not easily defeated by circumstances, 2) we receive the blessings of many Buddhas, 3) we are honored by human and heavenly beings, 4) we remember the Dharma easily, 5) we will know what we do not know, 6) we become effective in our use of language, 7) we attain deep meditative concentration , 8) we have fewer diseases and worries, 9) we improve our digestion, 10) we will become enlightened more quickly.

Diligence can be likened to starting a fire by rubbing two sticks together. If we keep at it, we will heat the wood enough to cause it to burn, while if we quit too soon, we will succeed only in making ourselves tired. Nearly everything in life is like this. If we stop too soon, we will fail to reach our goal. Most people are the same—they love the strong burst of enthusiasm that first comes when a new course of action is taken. But as time goes on and things become routine, they begin to lose interest and look for something else to inspire them. Diligence is founded on knowing that deep inspiration must come from within, for when we draw on our own inner resources, there is nothing that can stop us and nothing that can make us change course too soon.

There is a Buddhist story about a pair of parrots who saw a forest fire one day. Though the flames of the fire were fearsome, the parrots decided that they still must do whatever they could to stop the blaze. Accordingly, they began carrying water in their mouths from a river nearby. Though their efforts were insufficient to extinguish the blaze, the parrots kept at their labors. Seeing how determined they were, the god of fire spoke to them saying, "Parrots, why do you bother? You can never carry enough water to put out such a huge fire."

The parrots replied, "It is our duty to try anyway. If others would help us, we might even succeed in stopping the blaze."

When the god heard their answer, he was moved by their determination and put out the fire himself. This little story draws on a deep principle—when we are really determined to do something, powerful forces often will come to our aid. Diligence can unleash strengths in us that we never knew we had.

The *Sutra in Forty-Two Sections* says that there are three important stages in learning to be diligent: the protected stage, the stage of learning wholesome teachings, and the stage of working for the liberation of others. The protected stage corresponds to that period of time when we are first learning how to be diligent. During this stage we have to be careful about how we approach our task because our determination alone may not be strong enough to withstand all that we will have to bear. In this stage, we must appraise ourselves honestly as we clearly assess the difficulties that lie before us. Once we have understood what will be required of us, then we must shield ourselves from those things that might cause us to fail. For example, a student who is just beginning college must learn to avoid the use of drugs because if he does not, his grades will suffer and he may lose his way. A beginning teacher must be prepared to face the disappointment of not being able to help every student he teaches, for if he is not, he may become discouraged and quit teaching all together. When people are not prepared to shield themselves from disappointment and temptation, they too often lose heart and accomplish nothing at all. They may begin with great determination, but if they do not protect themselves properly, they may end up accomplishing nothing at all.

The second stage of diligence is the stage of learning wholesome teachings. Once we have learned to protect our resolve, we will begin to see more clearly the wholesome teachings that we can use to succeed at our chosen task. Once we are aware of the negative forces that we must avoid, we will be free to learn the wholesome teachings that will help us move forward. The shielded stage guards us from disappointment and negativity, while the learning stage allows us to acquire the skills that will help us to accomplish our goals. For example, if a beginning college student is successful in shielding himself from drug use, then he will be free to apply all of his energies to his studies. Similarly, if a beginning teacher is prepared for the inevitable disappointments that come with teaching, he will be in a better frame of mind to learn new methods that may produce better results.

The third stage of diligence is the stage of working for the liberation of others. No one is born with perfect diligence. All of us must learn to develop it at some time. The Buddha taught the three stages of its development because when we try to hurry our progress we too often fail. Don't wait to begin. One aspect of diligence is having a clear understanding that life is short and that we must use every opportunity to progress. Once the Buddha asked a group of disciples, "How much time do you have left to live?"

One disciple said, "We can only count on having a few more days."

The Buddha said, "No. Think some more."

Another disciple said, "We can only count on having enough time to finish our meal."

Again the Buddha said, "No. Think some more."

A third disciple said, "We can only count on a single breath."

The Buddha said, "Excellent! That is all the time we have."

When you place your attention on the moment, and on the very breath you are breathing now, can you still make excuses for laziness? Can you still find reasons to avoid doing what you know you must? Diligence is based on understanding that life is short and that we must make good use of all of the time that we have. If we do not act now, we will never succeed in "escaping the prison of the five aggregates and the three realms."

The following story can help us understand the importance of respecting ourselves enough to want to change for the better. Once Master Foyin was walking with the poet Su Dungpo when they came upon a stone statue of Guanyin. Master Foyin pressed his palms together and bowed to the statue.

Su Dungpo then said, "We bow to Guanyin because she can help us. But if this is so why does she hold mantra beads? If we contemplate her so that she will help us, who is she contemplating?"

Master Foyin replied, "This is a question you must ask yourself."

Su Dungpo said, "How can I answer that for myself?"

Master Foyin said, "Look at Guanyin. She is contemplating herself."

Su Dongpo said, "I know, but why would she contemplate herself?"

Master Foyin replied, "It is better to rely on yourself than to rely on others."

The Four Kinds of Mara

The main reason to study the Dharma is to learn how to break the hold of the troubles and cares that determine the lives of ordinary people. Our troubles are based on our harmful attachments and they work against us like thieves in the night, stealing all of the peace and contentment we have gathered over the years. The Buddha said that there are 84,000 kinds of delusion. In many of his talks he said that all of those kinds of delusion are based on nothing more than the three poisons of greed, anger, and ignorance. Our "prison" is nothing more than our own minds when they are filled with the three poisons.

In Buddhism the word *mara* generally means those parts of ourselves that work against our best interests. Understanding mara can be difficult because they are very hard to see. Just when we think that we are doing everything right, mara rises in our minds and tempts us toward excess.

In this section, the sutra employs the bold image of four kinds of mara holding us in the prison of the five aggregates and the three realms. Its injunction to escape our cramped cell stimulates our self-respect as it inspires us to greater diligence. The four kinds of mara conjured by this image are our afflictions, the five aggregates, death, and wrong views. Like jailors who are reflections of ourselves, these four kinds of mara confine us to a prison of our own devising. This use of strong imagery is not unusual in

Buddhist literature. Death is often referred to as mara or a soldier waiting by the door, while the five aggregates frequently are portrayed as fierce ghouls who rip tranquility and contentment from our lives, leaving us with nothing but pain.

On the night when the Buddha became enlightened, he was tempted and taunted by innumerable droves of maras that came to destroy his achievement, and haul his mind back to the interminable ordinariness of deluded life. In the *Sutra on the Past Vows of Ksitigarbha Bodhisattva* mara is described chasing and grabbing people who have been driven onto the shores of a caustic sea where they had been floating for days. With talons and fangs the mara tears flesh from the bodies of the beached swimmers as they drive them toward even deeper reaches of hell. In many sutras, people are described wailing and screaming as they boil in vats of oil or wander naked across freezing lands where there is no food and no relief from pain. Practitioners can make of these descriptions what they like. Some people take them literally; others see them as imaginative embellishments of our psychological fears and urges, while still others see them as artistic expansions on the notion that we are what we think we are and that all of us get exactly what we deserve. While it is surely not healthy to dwell on images as strong as these, it is not healthy either to completely ignore the horrors they suggest. Buddhism is a comprehensive religion of the mind, and it would be a falsification of its profundity to pretend that any part of life should be hidden from our awareness or kept in secret forever. We are what we are, and when we imagine otherwise we become as mara ourselves.

Once, a disciple said to Master Zhaozhou (779-897), "Master, you always behave with compassion and wisdom and you seem to have attained a state of perfect virtue. May I ask you, where will you be one hundred years from now?"

Zhaozhou said, "I'll be in hell!"

"What?" his disciple replied. "You are so virtuous why would you go to hell?"

Zhaozhou said, "To save you."

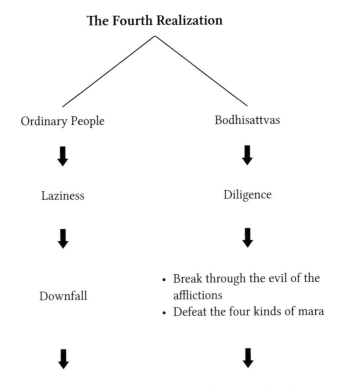

Chapter V

The Fifth Realization

Realize that ignorance gives rise to the cycle of birth and death. A bodhisattva is always mindful, studies widely, listens more, increases his wisdom, and becomes more eloquent in order to teach all beings great joy.

Chapter Five

The Fifth Realization
Study Widely, Listen More

How can we defeat our mara if we do not know that we have any? How can we overcome our ignorance if we pretend that we are wise? The first noble truth of Buddhism states that life is unsatisfactory and that all of us must experience pain and sorrow. Who can deny this truth? Realizing that this is so is the start of wisdom. The great mistake people make is to turn away from the Dharma because they want to turn away from themselves. They do not want to see the mara side of being. They do not want to know themselves. In their feigned perfection, their defilements, which grow like mushrooms in the dark, become only worse, for to ignore an unconscious condition of the mind is to increase it. We turn away from all that is good when we fail to account for that which is bad. This is why the Buddha counsels us to realize that "ignorance gives rise to the cycle of birth and death." In English the word ignorance is derived from the word "ignore." In Chinese ignorance literally means "without light," or "without understanding."

There can be no light in places we choose to ignore and there can be no understanding when we turn from the true nature of our human wants and fears.

A fundamental teaching of the Buddha is that the worlds we live in have been created by our own actions. Your family, your friends, your health, your needs, your nation, and everything else that you may call your own is truly your own because it was made by you. Your intentions and your karma brought it into being. "The cycle of birth and death" referred to in this section is the same as the "prison of the five aggregates and the three realms," which was mentioned in the last section. Calling it a cycle now is simply a more accurate way of describing how the prison is built and how it is filled again and again with the same beings whose endemic recidivism is the only cause of their confinement.

In the last section, the Buddha introduced the idea that we are imprisoned by the four maras of our afflictions, the five aggregates, death, and wrong views. It is important to understand what these maras are and what they mean to us if we truly hope to overcome the ignorance that gives rise to the cycle of birth and death and to escape from the prison of the five aggregates and the three realms.

The mara of our afflictions is everything within us that works to harm us or to harm others. This mara is especially vicious when we ignore it, or pretend that its urges are something other than what they are. The mara of our five aggregates is everything that allows us to believe that our individual awareness should be preeminent and above others. The face of this mara is everything that we vainly believe to be unique and important about ourselves. The mara of death is the brevity of any particular incarnation or the false appearance that it is hopeless to try to change.

The mara of wrong views is the mara of misunderstanding the Buddha's message. This is the mara that cajoles us to dismiss what we have not understood, or to turn away from that which does not flatter us. If we hope to gradually turn away from the cycle of birth and death, we must escape from the prison of ignorance that is guarded by these four powerful mara. This is why "A bodhisattva is always mindful, studies widely, listens more, increases his wisdom" and teaches the Dharma. The Buddha's central lessons cannot be learned in a day, or in a year, or even in a lifetime. They are not something to be noted and forgotten, but they are guides that must be consulted at all times.

Once there was a man who felt that he had been insulted by someone. He wanted to get even with the person who had offended him, but he could not think of how. He held his hatred in his heart and walked around feeling bitter and angry. One day a sorcerer asked him why he was so bitter. The man explained that he had been insulted and that he could not think of a good way to get even. The sorcerer said, "I know of a way to get even."

The man said, "Please tell me what it is."

The sorcerer said, "I know a curse that will kill the man you hate. However, I doubt that you will want to use it because one of the conditions of the curse is that if you use it, you will have to die too."

The man said, "I don't care! Tell me what it is!"

The sorcerer told him the curse and a few days later he learned that the man had died. All anger is like this. It always turns and harms us the most. Our minds control the ways that we react to the conditions of our lives. Ignorant behavior, as in the story above, arises in a mind that is dark and unaware of the depth of life. Contrast that story with the following one.

Master Ryokan lived very simply in a rude forest hut. One evening he returned from teaching the Dharma only to find that a thief was ransacking his hut.

Ryokan said, "You won't find anything in there. All I have are the clothes on my back." With that he took his clothes off and handed them to the thief. "Here take these," he said.

The thief clutched the clothing to his chest and ran away. As he disappeared into the night, Ryokan gazed toward the moon that shone down on his naked body. "How sad," he sighed, "that I cannot give him this beautiful moon as well."

Ignorance is that which causes us to be trapped in the cycle of birth and death. When we understand this cycle and our own parts in keeping it going, we will understand how to escape it. Buddhism is a religion that is made up of equal parts of wisdom and morality. Wisdom can be thought of as all that we know and understand about life, while morality can be thought of as the way that we behave, especially when our behavior impacts the lives of others. Buddhist wisdom is different from what most of us think of as learning or intellectual achievement, for the wisdom that the Buddha taught is always concerned with life and the many ways that we can benefit the beings living around us. The modern world presents us with many examples of "wisdom" that has caused more harm than good. People are capable of discovering marvelous inventions, but when these inventions are used to harm others their implementation cannot be called wise by any stretch of the imagination. True wisdom is deep insight into the nature of being. It is profound understanding of motive and intention. Wisdom is that which guides us to benefit both ourselves and others at the same time. It is that which leads us from the delusive cycle of birth and death.

In addition to the basic kinds of ignorance we have already discussed—greed, anger, pride and doubt—the Buddha also talked about several erroneous beliefs that frequently bind us to self-perpetuating cycles of harm and ignorance. These beliefs are particularly difficult to overcome because, though they are fallacious, they are founded on rational thinking processes.

The first erroneous belief is the belief that one's body is something that one actually possesses, and that this possession is something that must be clung to with all of one's strength. Even a cursory acquaintance with modern biology should lead us to understand that our bodies are composed of materials that we cannot control and that they are regulated by systems that we do not understand. How can we possibly hope to cling to this mysterious mélange of mysterious parts? It is not irrational to form the thought of wanting to cling to the body, but it becomes irrational to persist in this thought in the face of so much evidence against its possibility.

The second erroneous belief has two sides to it. On one side is the belief that life ends completely at death, while on the other side is the belief that an immortal soul continues to live after death. The Buddha said that both of these beliefs are wrong. Life does not end with the death of the physical body, but neither does some soul that now inhabits the body continue to live as if without interruption, in a disembodied state that must be immortal since it no longer is physical. The Buddha taught that when the body perishes, the karma that was generated by it continues on in a sort of "mind stream" that eventually gives rise to another life. This continuation is the essence of the cycle of birth and death.

The third erroneous belief is the belief that the Four Noble Truths are false, or that the world does not operate on a cause and effect basis. This belief all too often leads people to think that their actions do not have karmic effects and that it does not matter what they do or do not do. This belief can be very dangerous if it is entertained by someone with violent or anti-social tendencies.

The fourth erroneous belief is any belief that keeps one from understanding the Dharma. Any lower belief that clouds the mind or prevents higher learning is a serious detriment to continuing growth and development. Beliefs of this sort might be such ideas as dialectical materialism, fatalism, and nihilism.

The fifth erroneous belief is the belief in any religious practice that does not work. Fasting in order to gain psychic powers or committing suicide in order to go to heaven are examples of this.

Ignorance of the true nature of things can lead us to make many mistakes. The following story can be interpreted in many ways. Once, three Buddhist monks were traveling together along the banks of a slow moving stream. In the distance they could see a small village. The monks decided to go into the village to beg for alms. Just as they made their decision, one of them noticed a head of cabbage floating down the stream. He said, "We better not go to that village up there. Look how wasteful the villagers are. Someone has tossed a whole head of cabbage into the stream."

The other monks agreed. "There is no reason to preach the Dharma to people like that," they said.

Just then, a woman came running down the path toward them. "Masters," she cried, "Have you seen a cabbage floating in the stream? It fell out of my hands just a few minutes ago! It would be such a waste to lose it!"

With that the monks all looked at each other and said, "We better go there after all."

Sometimes the smallest things can lead to very different interpretations. Buddhist sutras generally describe ignorance as being a sort of darkness, but sometimes ignorance is nothing more than a small misunderstanding, or a small misinterpretation of the facts. The monks in the story above might have wandered for a long time before they found another village as good as the one they almost passed by.

Listening, Speaking

Master Taixu (1899-1947) once said, "The wisdom we gain from listening to the truth establishes our faith. The wisdom we gain from thinking about the truth establishes our morality. The wisdom we gain from practicing the truth establishes our relationship with the Buddha."

Master Taixu placed his statements in that order because to overcome ignorance we must first hear the truth. Having heard the truth, we must think about it. Having thought about it, we must practice it. This basic order is one that should be followed again and again as new aspects of the Dharma become clear to us. First we hear a new idea, then we think about it, then we apply it to our lives. If we fail to follow any of these steps, we will find it difficult to progress because our nascent wisdom will be weak in one of these important areas. Though this point is obvious, I rarely see people applying it as they should.

If we are to study widely and learn as much as we can about the Buddha's teaching, it follows that we must be open-minded. Close-mindedness or narrow sectarian thinking can only become a hindrance to real growth. Sometimes when people first begin to study Buddhism, they latch on to one small part of its vast tradition and refuse to consider that there can be other points of view, or that the truth can be seen from more than one angle. People like that often throw themselves into meditation or into one kind of Buddhist practice without recognizing that there are many ways to become enlightened. The Buddha never said to be close-minded or intolerant of practices that we do not understand!

In truth, it is very difficult to say exactly what the right way to practice Buddhism is; there are so many possibilities that we must be sure to keep our minds open to all of them, even as we focus on those aspects of the Dharma that we have chosen to perfect. Generally speaking, all Buddhist studies should be guided by the threefold training—morality, meditative concentration, and wisdom. The threefold training was described by the Buddha as a basic way to approach the Dharma, irrespective of what our personal inclinations may or may not be. The threefold training tells us to first to build a moral foundation, then to perfect our meditation and introspection, and lastly to become wise through these first two activities. Whether we are Esoteric, Theravadan, Chan, or Pure Land practitioners, all of us should rely on the threefold training as basic guidelines for our practice. Beyond that, we have the freedom to choose which sutras or which techniques we may want to study. We also have the freedom to choose those teachers that we feel will benefit us the most. In choosing one way over another, however, we should never allow ourselves to lose respect for other people who may have made decisions that are different from our own.

The *Suramgama Sutra* describes the exquisite listening ability of Avalokitesvara, whose name means "he who listens to the sound of the world." His listening ability is described as having three wonderful aspects—it is able to penetrate the truth, contain the truth, and remember the truth. Penetrating the truth means that his power to listen and understand cannot be blocked by anything. Unlike eyesight, which may be blocked by a wall, his listening abilities cannot be hindered by anything. Containing the truth means that his listening abilities are not confined to only one angle at a time. Unlike eyesight which can only see one side of a thing at a time, Avalokitesvara can hear everything in all directions at once, and thus he "contains" them all. Remembering the truth means that what he heard in the past, he still remembers today. Our hearing may penetrate anything and contain everything, but if we do not remember, it will be as if we had heard nothing at all. All Buddhists should model themselves on Avalokitesvara as much as possible. There is nothing anywhere that we should not seek to learn and understand.

When we have succeeded in acquiring listening abilities like Avalokitesvara, we will become more eloquent and teach all beings with great joy. Eventually our eloquent abilities should be as unobstructed as our listening abilities, for only when we understand how to expound the Dharma will we be able to help others learn to see the truth. This kind of eloquent ability should not be confused with the ability to argue or debate, for the purpose of this skill is only to lead people toward the truth, not to defeat them or win anything from them. This kind of skill is acquired by first listening to others and understanding their hopes and fears, then slowly learning how to respond to them in such a way that our words can be a help to them. Ultimately, we would hope that our words will "transform them" by leading them to a deeper understanding of the Dharma. Talking too much is another habit that should be avoided when trying to learn the skill of transforming others with our words. Deep transformation is always an intensely personal inner process. In most cases, we will bring more benefit by listening to others than by talking to them. A few well placed words will always be more valuable than hours of babbling. Once the great philosopher Socrates was enrolling students in an informal class he was giving on public speaking. The fee for the class was ten cents. A young man came to register for the class, and as he was doing so he explained at great length why he wanted to learn to become a good speaker, what the value of speaking was, and so on. After he at last stopped speaking, Socrates asked him to pay an additional ten cents. The student was shocked to hear this and asked him why he was being required to pay twice as much as the other people in the class.

Socrates said, "The other students are paying ten cents to learn how to talk, but you must pay twenty cents because not only do I have to teach you how to talk, I also must teach you how to stop talking."

Buddhist sutras generally mention four important aspects of eloquence. Though these aspects are ideals that are beyond the reach of most of us most of the time, they still are very good indications of what the Buddha meant when he said to "become more eloquent to teach all beings to reach great joy."

The first aspect is called the "unobstructed eloquence of the Dharma." *Unobstructed* means that there is nothing preventing us from seeing and knowing what is denoted by the words of the Buddha. If our speaking talents are based on an unblocked eloquence of the Buddha's words, we will be able to know how to answer any question that is put to us. The second aspect is called "unobstructed eloquence of the principles underlying the Dharma." It is one thing to know what the words mean, but it is another thing to understand the deep principles upon which they are based. The third aspect is called "unobstructed eloquence of the expression." This means that we are able to express the truths of the Dharma in terms that are well suited to our audience. The fourth aspect is called "unobstructed eloquence of joy in teaching the Dharma." We may possess the first three aspects, but if we lack the fourth, few people will benefit from our talents.

The important thing to remember about developing your speaking talents is that these talents are not something that should be used to lord over others, defeat them in verbal debates, or bore them with endless droning. Deep and effective speaking abilities rely as much on silence and listening as they do on actual speech.

The *Vimalakirti Sutra* contains a famous passage that illustrates this idea very well. Once, a large group of very advanced disciples of the Buddha went to visit Vimalakirti. The subject of "the Dharma door of non-duality" arose, and the group discussed it from many different angles. When someone asked Manjusri what his thoughts were. Manjusri said, "In my view, going beyond duality means going beyond all phenomenal appearances, beyond all questions and answers, beyond all words, all speech, and all analytical thought processes."

When he was finished speaking, Manjusri asked Vimalakirti what he thought. Vimalakirti looked at him and said nothing.

Without using a single word, Vimalakirti revealed that of all the learned people who were present, his speaking abilities were paramount, for when we truly go beyond duality, we also go beyond all words and all descriptions.

In contrast, but not in contradiction, to this story from the *Vimalakirti Sutra*, there is the story of Master Zhiyi (538-597) who once spoke for three whole months on the first word of the Chinese title of the *Lotus Sutra*. Great speakers simply know when to speak at length and when to remain silent. Sometimes a long lecture is just the thing, sometimes a smile is all that is needed. The main reason to develop eloquence is to help others and lead them to the great joy of understanding the truth for themselves.

The *Sutra in Forty-Two Sections* says, "One who sees the Way is like someone who has brought a torch into a dark room—suddenly the darkness is gone and all that remains is light. If we study the Way and see the truth, our ignorance will disappear and light will appear everywhere." More than anything else, Buddhism is a religion of wisdom; the wisdom that arises when we see ourselves as we really are.

The Fifth Realization

Ordinary People

↓

Ignorance

↓

The Cycle of Birth and Death

Five Afflictions:
- Greed
- Anger
- Ignorance
- Pride
- Doubt

Wrong Views:
- Views of the body
- Extreme views
- Evil views
- Views that attach to wrong views as truth
- Views attached to immorality

Bodhisattvas

Benefit Others

↓

Giving All Beings Great Joy

↙ ↘

Liberate Sentient Beings

Teach all beings throughout the Dharma realms.

Teach the Dharma

Develop unobstructed eloquence of Dharma, principles, expression, and joy.

Benefit Oneself

↙ ↘

Opening Wisdom

↓

Listen More

Three wisdoms of listening, thinking, and practice

Seeking Liberation

↓

Study Widely

Threefold training of morality, meditative concentration, and wisdom

Chapter VI

The Sixth Realization

Realize that those who are poor and suffering have more resentment, and that this leads them to create unwholesome conditions. A bodhisattva practices giving and has equal concern for friend and foe. He does not recollect past unwholesome deeds committed against him, nor does he hate unwholesome people.

Chapter Six

The Sixth Realization
The Importance of Practicing Giving

This realization concerns our attitudes toward poverty and wealth. There are two basic things to understand about the meaning of this realization. The first is that neither poverty nor wealth is a permanent state of being; sometimes poor people become wealthy and sometimes wealthy people lose everything they have. No material condition is permanent. The second important thing to understand about this realization is that the dualistic pair—poverty and wealth—can have many different meanings. The Buddha is not just talking about material poverty and wealth, but also about intellectual, moral, and spiritual poverty and wealth. All of us surely have known someone who was spiritually wealthy though materially poor. And most have probably also seen the opposite of this kind of person—someone who is materially very wealthy, but spiritually mean and angry. Karmic fruits should never be understood in terms of a debased equation wherein the quantity of one's material possessions is believed to indicate the degree of one's virtue. Material wealth and spiritual wealth are not produced by the same conditions or the same energies.

The sutra says that "those who are poor and suffering have more resentment, and that this leads them to create unwholesome conditions." This is so because when we are resentful, we tend to blame others for our suffering, while ignoring its deeper causes. Poor people who resent the wealthy would do much better if they used their energies to create conditions that were not so disagreeable. Wealthy people who resent poor people or who hold society in contempt are only planting the seeds of their eventual downfall. All of us must learn to live together and help each other during the brief period of time that we inhabit this realm.

Resentment is a low emotion caused by dwelling on the negative features of a situation without doing anything about them. People who are resentful usually blame others for problems that are really their own. There are four basic kinds of resentment mentioned in Buddhist sutras. The first is resenting the heavens for one's "fate." This sort of resentment frequently leads people to adopt perverse religious views in order to change their fates, or to appease the gods that they believe are persecuting them. The second kind of resentment is directed toward the social system or the environment. People blame the economic system, the political system, the climate, or the land for their problems. The third is resenting one's family or taking one's resentments out on family members. A great deal of domestic violence and abuse is caused when people blame their loved ones for conditions that are beyond their control. The fourth is resenting our friends for not helping us when we should be helping ourselves.

The *Path of Practice Sutra* says, "Those who want to improve themselves should realize that when they turn their anger on others, they are hurting themselves most of all. They are like sticks of wood using fire to attack others; in the end they burn themselves the most." The *Sutra on the Samadhi of Great Merit* says, "Rid yourself of passion and hate, and do not let yourself be resentful or mean. Practice compassion and look upon your enemies as your friends."

Nowhere has it been said that we should not recognize social or political problems when they exist, or that we should not strive to make the best of a poor environment. The meaning of this realization is not that we should passively accept everything that happens to us, but that we should work to change bad conditions through acts of kindness and giving, and that we should not allow ourselves to become angry or resentful while doing so. Resentment is an inner state that we have the power to control. It is a sign of ignorance and "harmful attachment." If we feel that we are susceptible to feelings of resentment, we should strive to monitor our moods and behavior. The moment we find ourselves feeling resentful, we should stop and reflect on what is causing our mood and why we are choosing to indulge in this negative state.

The single best cure for all mental and emotional defilements is to emphasize their positive opposites. At first this sort of emphasis can feel contrived and unsatisfying, but in time we will see that it produces very good results, for it is based on the deep principles that underlie all of our mental functions. The mind works in dualistic pairs; anger is the polar opposite of love or kindness, passion is the opposite of reason, fear is the opposite of trust. When we fall under the spell of any emotional state, we must look to balance it by bringing forth its opposite. If we find ourselves indulging in resentment, we must try to be as reasonable and compassionate as we can. At first, this behavior may feel strained, but in a very short time it will lead us to a much healthier state of mind. If we are honest with ourselves, we will soon conclude that our resentment was nothing more than a harmful attachment to a false appearance and that persisting in it would not have brought any good results at all. Indeed, an ongoing cycle of resentment and anger can lead to violent explosions that are far out of proportion to the imaginary "offenses" that started them in the first place. Daily, there are stories in the paper about these kinds of violent eruptions. As we shake our heads in wonder at them, we should also remember that nearly all of them began as some small irritation that someone allowed to grow into a boil of resentment, and then from there into an angry crime scene. Is it any wonder that the Buddha called such moods mara? Or that Buddhist art for centuries has depicted mara as a warning to our subconscious, as well as to our conscience? As long as we are alive, none of us should dare to stop monitoring our moods and feelings for signs of resentment or anger. Harmful attachments are generally not dangerous if we identify them in time and take proper measures to eradicate them. When we fail to notice them, or when we lie to ourselves about their true natures, however, they can grow very quickly into horrendous monsters that have the capacity to ruin all the good that we have ever done.

The following story reminds us that only wisdom can overcome ignorance, and that it is impossible to run away from ourselves. Once there was a sage who agreed to teach three young students the way to enlightenment. Fearing that they might be lured from the path by the glitter of the world, the sage took his students to a place deep in the mountains, where he taught them for many years. When the boys reached the age of sixteen, the sage decided that it was time to take them into a city to show them what life in the world was really like. No sooner did they enter the city, than the sage noticed that his students were fascinated by the beautiful women that were walking everywhere. To keep their minds on the truth, the sage said, "Be careful of them for they are not what they seem. They are man-eating tigers!"

They continued touring the city. They visited temples and shrines, and called on several renowned masters. At nightfall the sage led them back to the mountains. When they were safe in their retreat once again, he asked, "What did you learn today? What was the most interesting thing you saw?"

Without hesitation the three replied in unison, "The man-eating tigers!"

We cannot run from who we are. That sage would have done better to raise the boys in a town where they would have learned to understand themselves from an early age. We must learn to free ourselves from the attachments of our minds, not to run from them or pretend that they can be ignored.

This sixth realization counsels us to *practice giving and have equal concern for friend and foe.* Equal concern for friend and foe is the balance point at the center of the mind's constellations of dualistic emotions. When first glimpsed, this point may seem very small, but after we have visited it often, we will realize that it actually contains the entire universe. Even mindedness is the goal of Buddhist morality, the basis of Buddhist meditation, and the fruit of Buddhist wisdom. It is the portal to the Buddha mind, the essence of enlightenment, and the fulfillment of all that we are. Buddhism is often called the "Middle Way" in honor of the great rewards that can be gained by equal concern. When we have concern we do not see a distinction between friend and foe, we do not notice resentment, and we do not feel selfish. Deep concern is a positive state that rests in the knowledge that all beings are one and that giving is the only natural state of the heart.

The *Sutra on the Three Dharmas of Great Wisdom* says, "If you want to become enlightened, have equal concern for all sentient beings." The *Moon Lamp Samadhi Sutra* says, "To have equal concern for all things means that there is no sense of this or that, or of discriminating or not discriminating, or of doing something, or of giving rise to something, or of creating something, or of extinguishing something. All delusion, all analytical thought, and all ideas are simply stopped."

Giving

Giving is a very important virtue. Coupled with patience, it is basic to all social activity. Giving is that virtue which reaches out to others, while patience is that which allows us to tolerate the unkindness with which we may be met. The Buddha said that the six most important virtues of a bodhisattva are giving, morality, patience, diligence, meditative concentration, and wisdom.

Once during the time of the Buddha there was a woman who was very poor. She went to Katyayana and explained her plight and asked him what she should do. Katyayana said that she should stop worrying because he knew of a way to change her situation. The woman begged him to tell her what it was.

Katyayana said, "Sell your poverty to others!"

"Sell it?" the woman asked. "If people bought poverty, why soon there would be no poverty in the world! And who would want to buy someone else's poverty anyway?"

Katyayana said, "Sell it to me."

The woman said, "I don't know how to sell it. What should I do?"

Katyayana said, "All you have to do is give to everyone. That is the way to sell poverty."

"You see," he continued, "In your last life you were never generous with anyone. You hoarded everything and never gave anything to anyone. So now you are poor. If you can learn to give, you will see that your situation will quickly change."

When he finished speaking, the woman realized that Katyayana had indeed told her the truth. In just a few moments she had learned how to eradicate her poverty, as well as how to be a good bodhisattva, which is far more important.

This realization asks us to practice giving. Some might wonder how a poor woman is supposed to give. Isn't giving something that only rich people can do? The answer to this question is no. Giving comes from a deep state of mind that is based on the recognition that the well being of others is fully as important as our own. There are many ways to practice giving, not just one. We can be give our time, our wisdom, our skills, and our willingness to listen to others, with encouragement, and so on. Material giving is important, and no Buddhist temple would ever have been built without it, but this is not the only way to give.

Buddhist sutras generally recognize three important kinds of giving: material giving, emotional giving, and the giving of the Dharma. Each of these forms of giving is two-sided. On the one side our giving helps others, while on the other side it helps us. Properly practiced, giving teaches us to be compassionate toward others, broad minded in our view of the world, and unattached to our own possessions or points of view. Though material giving begins on the material plane, it almost always rises above that. Gifts of money or goods show others that we care about them and want them to be happy. Material gifts to schools and temples help others benefit from the Dharma, while donations to Buddhist organizations help fund the work of translating Buddhist literature and educating the next generation of Buddhist practitioners.

Fearless giving means giving of ourselves. The Buddha described this form of giving as teaching others not to be afraid. Fear is the great unrecognized emotion. It leads us to selfishness, anger, resentment, cowardice and many other negative states of mind. The Buddha taught the Dharma to help us learn to stop being afraid. Once we understand the conditions of life, we will no longer fear them, for we will know how to use them to our advantage.

The greatest kind of giving is teaching others the Dharma, for only the Dharma can show them how to free themselves from all forms of suffering. Though this is the greatest kind of giving, it should be recognized that Dharma giving cannot really be separated from material or emotional giving. In the best cases, the three kinds of giving are simply three parts of the same act. For example, when we enter a temple, we receive the gift of other's material giving. When we experience the tranquility of the Buddha hall, we receive the gift of their emotional giving. And when we learn something of the Dharma inside the temple, we experience their gift of the truth. The people that built that temple for our use gave us a gift that will touch every part of our being if we are receptive to it and willing to receive it.

At its deepest level a perfect act of giving dwells in conscious emptiness, in the awareness that each of the three components of the act of giving is without absolute substance. This means that one is aware in a very deep sense that there is no giver, no gift, and no recipient of any gift. This level of awareness is not the same as merely thinking that nothing is happening, for the spiritual energy that inspires the giver to include the recipient in a selfless act is very real. Indeed, this spiritual energy is a manifest aspect of the Buddha mind that underlies all conscious acts. The profound compassion that leads to acts of deep giving is an aspect of the Buddha that dwells within. A glimpse of this compassion is an intimation of the depth of awareness that is our true potential, and the true nature of our beings. In this sense, compassion and giving can be understood as windows through which we view the Buddha himself. Ultimately, this view will lead to a state of being in which the viewer is absorbed into the view, in which the deluded self is led to understand that the real basis of its being is immensely greater than anything it had ever been able to conceive on its own. Sakyamuni Buddha taught the importance of compassion and giving for their intrinsic value, but also because experiencing these states is the surest means of all to experience the Buddha who is the one truth and the knower of all.

Do Not Recollect Past Unwholesome Deeds

Not recollecting past unwholesome deeds is also a form of giving, as well as wisdom, for when we dwell on negative memories we often become resentful or angry, and these states just lead toward more of the same. The cycle of birth and death can be seen in the large picture of one lifetime after another, but it can also be seen in the details of one life. Recollecting past unwholesome deeds eventually leads to new unwholesome deeds, that quickly become old unwholesome deeds in someone else's mind. Returning anger with anger, seeking revenge, brooding about the past, refusing to forgive—all of these are actions that perpetuate the cycle of suffering and pain. Most evil is caused by people reacting negatively to something unwholesome they perceive that someone has done them. The way to stop this cycle is to take responsibility for your part in it. As much as you can, forgive and forget, and do not dwell on the people that you believe have harmed you. Not only will you benefit, but so will society in general. During the time of the Buddha, Devadatta tried to harm the Buddha several times—by telling lies about him, by attacking him with a drunken elephant, and by shoving a stone down a hill at him. The Buddha never once responded with anger or resentment to any of these acts. Instead, he said, "Devadatta is only helping me by urging me forward. He is my great teacher." If you can see your "foes" who have done wrong to you as your "great teachers," you will have understood this realization and more, for forgiveness of this magnitude is always followed by an enormous upsurge in joy and good fortune. When we break the chains of the past like this, we actually change the conditions and direction of our karma.

While most of us realize that it is best not to "recollect past unwholesome deeds committed against us," few of us are able to do this. The right way to let go of the past is to benefit from it. Rather than resent something that we perceive as an "unwholesome deed," we should look at it more closely and discover how it may help us. No one grows spiritually who experiences nothing. Set-backs and hardships can and should be used to train us and spur us on to new achievements. Countries that have only one political party stagnate, while those that have functioning democratic institutions do not. Bodies that never get any exercise become weak, while those that are forced to strain themselves grow strong and healthy. Hardship is nothing more than our perception of one side of a dualistic pair. Whenever we find ourselves being challenged by hardship, we should consider how it strengthens us and helps us. When others insult us, or complain about us, or treat us badly, we should accept them as teachers who can help us become stronger and wiser. "Past unwholesome deeds" are nothing more than old lessons that we have not yet fully learned. To resent them is to compound the problem that brought them on in the first place.

The following story shows how important our attitudes can be. Once there was a man who was very curious about the difference between heaven and hell. He knew that beings in heaven were very happy and that those in hell were very unhappy. One day, he met a sage who told him that he could take him to both heaven and hell so that he could see for himself what the differences between them were. The man said that he was ready to go immediately.

Suddenly, the sage transported them to hell. The man was surprised at first because the scene before him was very similar to a scene on earth. A group of people were seated at a table eating dinner. When he looked more closely, however, he saw that the people were using chopsticks that were three feet long. Since the chopsticks were so long, the people at the table kept bumping each other and dropping their food. No one was getting enough to eat and everyone was very irritable and nasty.

Suddenly the scene changed, and the man knew that he was in heaven. But once again he was surprised at what he saw. Before him there was a group of people not all that different from the group he had seen in hell. This group, too, was seated at a table eating dinner, and they, too, were using chopsticks that were three feet long. When the man looked more closely, however, he saw that instead of dropping their food and becoming irritable as the beings in hell had been doing, the heavenly beings were using their long chopsticks to feed each other. Everyone was laughing and smiling and they were all getting plenty to eat.

The Sixth Realization

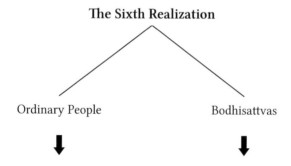

Ordinary People

Creates unwholesome conditions

⬇

Blame and Resentment

- Gods
- Society
- Family
- Friends

Bodhisattvas

Has equal concern for friend and foe. Does not recollect past unwholesome deeds committed against him, nor does he hate unwholesome people.

⬇

Three Kinds of Giving

- **Material Giving**: The gift of material things to help other people

- **Dharma Giving**: The gift of knowledge and truth

- **Emotional Giving**: The gift of support and comfort

Chapter VII

The Seventh Realization

Realize that wrongdoing comes from the five desires. Even though you are an ordinary person, do not be stained by worldly pleasures. Always be mindful of the triple robe, the bowl, and dharma instruments, and be willing to leave home, uphold the Way purely, practice the holy life well, and have compassion for all beings.

Chapter Seven

The Seventh Realization
Morality Fosters Self-control

In the second realization, the Buddha explained that "more desire causes more suffering," and that the way to overcome this problem is to "lessen desire and be without any wishes and the body and mind will be at ease." He also says that "the weariness of the cycle of birth and death arises from greed and desire." In this seventh realization, the topic again is desire, but the focus of the Buddha's comments is slightly different. Morality is now the means to overcome the "five desires." Since basic Buddhist morality is concerned mainly with restraint, the shift in focus between these two realizations may not be as great as it first seems. This realization can be thought of as a more detailed explanation of how to control excessive desire.

Most people believe that morality confines them while the five desires set them free. We shall see in a moment why this is not true.

Roughly speaking the five desires are the desire for wealth, sex, fame, food, and sleep. In a more philosophical context, they can also be understood to be any sensual craving associated with seeing, hearing, smelling, tasting, or touching. However we define them, the five desires of this realization are material desires that are wholly of this world.

This is why the Buddha also says "though you are an ordinary person, do not be stained by worldly pleasures." The way to enlightenment requires dedication to the beings of this world, but not to the incidental sensual pleasures that may arise from this dedication. It is easy for a bodhisattva to fail in this area because as his concern for others grows, his ability to attract people to him also grows. Though the *Eight Realizations of a Bodhisattva Sutra* is aimed at lay disciples, the Buddha evokes the image of a monk in this realization to remind us of how we should think about our place in the world. While outwardly we may resemble ordinary people, inwardly we should think of ourselves as monks who have renounced the five desires and all of the worldly pleasures that are associated with them. The five desires are seductive. That is why we need the Dharma to help us avoid becoming entangled in them.

Worldly cravings are characterized by the way they draw us in and then trap us in a complex tangle of unpleasant options and disagreeable outcomes. Who has not experienced this kind of trouble? The first Noble Truth says that life is unsatisfactory or that it is marked by inevitable suffering. The five desires are those energies that draw us only deeper into this level of reality. You may deny the first Noble Truth when you believe that it is convenient for you to do so, but your denial one day will be seen for what it really was—a convenience that allowed you to indulge in something you would have been better off leaving alone. The older we get, the more self-evident this truth becomes. Most of us discover the depths of the first Noble Truth through a mixture of hearing about it and experiencing it for ourselves. Only after we are convinced of its validity, will we be ready to learn the second Noble Truth—the origin of suffering.

The origin of all suffering can be found among the "three poisons" of greed, anger, and ignorance. The five desires are a more detailed description of greed. Greed, anger, and ignorance are called the three poisons because they kill spiritual joy and ruin goodness.

The five desires draw us in by a kind of selective hypnosis that emphasizes certain details of our cravings while ignoring others. If we crave wealth, we see only what we can buy, how others will be impressed with us, or how we will be able to avoid life's inconveniences. We do not see how we will become cold or arrogant, how we will isolate ourselves from others, or how we will ultimately become dull because we have ceased to have experiences that deepen us. When we emphasize excitement, we fail to see the sorrow that trails just behind. When we emphasize pride, we fail to see the shame we cause. When we emphasize power, we fail to see the misery that must ensue from its inevitable misuses. If we crave sex, we tend to emphasize the beauty of the person we desire, the loneliness we feel without them, and the joy that we will feel when we are with them. When passion rises in the breast, who thinks of the day when it must cool? The desire to have fame is an exaggeration of the normal urge to be socially acceptable or to have a good reputation. Ironically, this exaggeration contradicts itself for fame all too often is acquired by harming the very people we would like to have approve of us.

Generally speaking, each of the five desires can be understood as an exaggeration of a normal and valuable human need. The desire for wealth is an exaggeration of the normal desire to have a safe home and an adequate income. The desire for sex is an exaggeration of the normal urge to have a loving partner and a family. Overeating is an exaggeration of the normal desire to nourish the body, while excessive sleeping or laziness (in the absence of disease) is an exaggeration of a normal need to rest.

When we gaze upon our needs with a balanced sense of wisdom, we will be far less likely to be seduced by any one of them. Most of us have control of at least some of our basic human urges. If we can apply the reasoning that gives us control over these urges to all of the five desires, we will go a long way toward discovering the equal concern of the Buddha's Middle Way. Desire is not wrong in and of itself, if it is kept in proportion. When it is allowed to grow into a "poison," however, it will always lead to suffering.

The *Avatamsaka Sutra* says, "Sentient beings pass through the long night of their many lives dreaming of the five desires, following the five desires, greedily clinging to the five desires. Their minds are set on them and so they continuously indulge in weakness and remain trapped in the cycle of birth and death." The *Sutra of Fathers and Sons* says, "As soon as we understand the problems caused by the five desires, we will want to disentangle ourselves from them. Nothing in the world is greater than wisdom that cleanses the mind of desire."

Greed can be further analyzed into the five desires and the troubles caused by these desires can be further analyzed into five basic types. The first trouble is an increase in conflict. When we indulge in any of the five desires, we tend to have more conflicts with the people around us. The second trouble is an increased sense of nervousness or anxiety. The five desires strain our normal capacities to the point where we begin to feel unsettled and ill at ease no matter where we are or what we are doing. The third trouble is a tendency to harm others. As desire pulls us deeper into its delusional realm, we run the risk of harming others to gain more for ourselves. The fourth trouble is we become unrealistic. As desire increases, our thinking tends to become fantastic or impractical; we lose the sense of well-grounded reason that is so important to the spiritual path. The fifth trouble is we become inconsistent and flighty. A desire that has been thwarted here leads us to seek there for its elusive reflection in yet some other impossible scheme. We run from one thing to the next in pursuit of something that does not even exist.

Desire is like honey on the blade of a knife. If we are careful about sampling it because we know that the sharp edge is there, we will probably not harm ourselves. But if we are ignorant of its true nature, we will surely cut ourselves on the steel that lies concealed beneath the sweetness. This is why the Buddha counsels us to keep the image of a monk in our minds. As we live in the world, we must be careful to control what we hope to gain for ourselves, for if we allow ourselves to slide into a life of greed and craving, there is no guarantee that we will be able to free ourselves from it soon. The best way to deal with desires and prevent them from becoming excessive is to frequently take stock of ourselves in the light of the five precepts. The five precepts are no killing, no stealing, no lying, no sexual misconduct, and no use of drugs or alcohol. If we find that we are beginning to violate any of these basic precepts, we must conclude that one, or more of the five desires, is beginning to take root in our life. The moment we discover this, we should begin to use the four contemplations discussed in the chapter on the first realization. These contemplations were designed by the Buddha to help us gain mental control over the kinds of problems created by the five desires.

As we progress in spiritual studies, there comes a point when we realize that morality is not something that confines us or limits us, but that it is the only means we have to truly become free. By using morality to learn a more enlightened kind of behavior, we free ourselves from the complications that inevitably result from a life devoted to indulgence and sensual pleasure. The Buddha's teachings on morality are an inestimable gift for they help us to discover who we really are.

Once there was a king who got lost while riding one day. As he was searching for the road back to his palace, he came upon an old house. Since the king was thirsty, he went up to the house and knocked on the door. A woman's face appeared in a window, but she did not open the door.

The king called to her saying, "Why don't you open the door?"

The woman replied, "Because I have no clothes to wear."

With that, the king took off his robe and handed it to the woman in the window. To his surprise, as soon as she touched the robe, it burst into flames. The king thought that was strange, but he didn't say anything. Instead he removed his jacket and handed that to the woman. But the same thing happened again. As soon as she touched it, it burst into flames. The king said, "What is happening? As soon as you touch my clothes, they burst into flames."

The woman said, "Last night I had a dream that you would be coming today. In my dream, I saw that I had been your queen in a former life. But during that time, I was very greedy. Whenever, you wanted to donate food or clothing to the monastery, I would always complain and say that you should spend the money on me instead. That is why in this life, I can't wear any clothes at all. As soon as I touch them, they turn to flames."

The king asked, "Is there something I can do to help you?"

The woman replied, "In my dream I saw that if you were to give some clothing to a saint in my name, then I would be able to wear clothes again."

The king did as she asked. And only after that was the woman able to wear clothes.

Greed and immorality exact a price that we rarely see at the time. This is why this realization counsels us to be content with what we have. When we always try to get more for ourselves, we plant seeds that one day will grow into circumstances that are much more difficult for us.

The sutra says that we should always be mindful of "the triple robe, the bowl, and the dharma instruments." We provide ourselves with an easily remembered standard of behavior when we hold the image of a monk in our minds. By thinking often of the monastic way of life, we provide ourselves with a stable point of view from which to view life in this world. If we form the habit of often thinking like a monk, we will be much less likely to indulge in desire the next time we are tempted. With his conscience clear and his needs simple, a monk has the freedom to soar beyond this world and the troubles that are caused by living with greed, anger, or ignorance.

A monk's robe is a symbol of the material simplicity of his life. His bowl is a symbol of his well regulated needs. And his dharma instruments are a symbol of his dedication to teaching and learning the Dharma as long as there is still breath in his body. He must be willing to leave home, uphold the Way purely, practice the holy life well, and have compassion for all beings. This line recalls the dedication of a monk and counsels us to follow his example whenever we are able. Once we have internalized this image of monastic purity and understood the fullness of it, we will be well prepared to face the temptations of the five desires, whenever they may arise. In this context, I would encourage all of my readers to seek out monastic communities whenever possible. The people living in them are not all perfect, but each of them has given his life to the well being of sentient beings. The Buddha created a monastic institution, and he asked all of his followers to respect it and learn from it. The Buddha is the doctor, the Dharma is the medicine, and the Sangha are the nurses. You will gain much from having contact with monks and nuns for they are the direct spiritual descendents of the Buddha's first disciples.

Even as we respect Buddhist monks and nuns, it is important to realize that not every spiritual aspirant need become one. Buddhist history is full of stories of many non-monastics who achieved enlightenment. The important distinction to make is not whether someone has become a monk or not, but the depth of his commitment to the Dharma. While almost anyone can shave his head, only a few people can honestly give their whole minds to the truth. There are four basic ways that we can understand monastic life and the commitment it entails. In the first way, both the mind and the body are dedicated to the renunciation of worldly pleasures. When a person is dedicated in this way, he makes a very good monk. In the second way, the mind is dedicated to renunciation, but the body is not. When a person is of this type, he becomes a very good Buddhist practitioner, but he does not become a monk. In the third way, the body is dedicated to renunciation, but the mind is not. This kind of person, though he has become a monk in appearance, is not yet ready to give his whole being to his calling; he still holds many worldly desires and thoughts. In the fourth way, neither the body nor the mind is dedicated to renunciation. Though we must always try to help people of this type, it is also important to not allow ourselves to be overly influenced by their ways of thinking. People like this still believe that the deluded projections of their own harmful attachments contain all that is valuable in life. Needless to say, nothing could be farther from the truth.

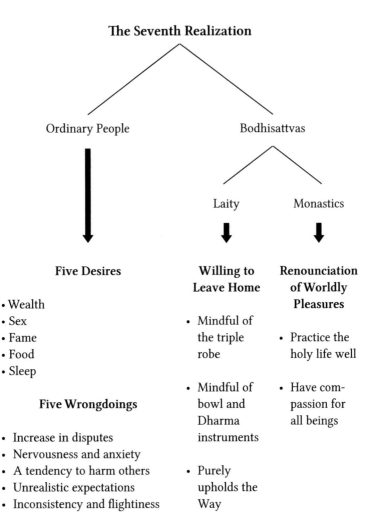

Chapter VIII

The Eighth Realization

Realize that the cycle of birth and death is a raging fire and that suffering is boundless. Initiate the Mahayana mind to universally help all beings and vow to shoulder the boundless suffering of sentient beings so that all sentient beings may reach great joy.

Chapter Eight

The Eighth Realization
The Mahayana Mind

It is no small thing to "vow to shoulder the boundless suffering of sentient beings so that all sentient beings reach great joy." Simply contemplating a vow of this magnitude improves us. Imagining the millions of sentient beings before us who made this vow is an experience that is as humbling as it is inspiring. Vowing to shoulder the boundless suffering of sentient beings means "to suffer for them, with them, and in place of them." The purpose of doing this is so that all sentient beings may reach great joy. This is the core of Mahayana Buddhism. One stands before it in awe. This vow is a crucible that will change the world. It is the key to enlightenment. It is the absolute center of the Buddha mind. The *Avatamsaka Sutra* says, "Make the great and compassionate vow to liberate all sentient beings, and not to leave one of them behind."

The first realization of this sutra deals with the Buddha's view of this world. The second through the seventh realizations deal with the Buddha's views on human life. This last realization is the most important one in the sutra for in this one the Buddha provides us with his highest level of instruction. The first seven realizations of this sutra concern what might be called the Buddha's philosophy of life. This last realization concerns his answer to that philosophy. Buddhism sometimes is misinterpreted as a passive or negative religion that counsels its followers to withdraw from life. This last realization should be sufficient proof that the Buddha never intended his teachings to be understood in that way. Not only did Sakyamuni Buddha ask us to vow to take on the sufferings of others, he also showed us how to do this by the example of his own life. Following his enlightenment, the Buddha spent forty-five years teaching others how to liberate themselves from delusion. The entire second half of his life in this world was dedicated to taking on the sufferings of others.

The Buddha taught that merely understanding the abstract doctrines of no-self, emptiness, impermanence, suffering, and nirvana is not enough. Buddhism is not a religion of mere abstractions. All of the ideas discussed in this sutra are meant to be used; they are meant to be used in the task of leading all sentient beings to be joyful. This task is begun by understanding the philosophical aspects of the Buddha's teachings, but it is only completed by implementing those teachings.

All Buddhas and bodhisattvas have vowed to universally help all beings and shoulder their boundless suffering so that they may attain great joy. This basic vow is known as a "general vow." The specific ways that different Buddhas enact this vow are known as their "specific vows." The vows that Buddhas make commit them to something, but they also give them a sort of power that is called the "power of the vow." This power arises from the fact that their vows create forces that are unimaginable to ordinary people. Entire Buddha realms can come into being on the strength of a single vow. A vow thus can also be called a "basic cause" of someone becoming a Buddha. When the forces of the mind all are marshaled toward the same goal, there is nothing that can prevent success. The only thing that can limit the power of a conscious vow are the unconscious forces of greed, anger, pride, doubt, and ignorance, for only these forces can cause the mind to fall back into its customary tangle of harmful attachments.

The vow to universally help all beings and shoulder their boundless suffering so that they may attain great joy is often called the "Mahayana vow." *Mahayana* means "large vehicle." Mahayana Buddhist practice is centered on the good of all sentient beings; it is based on the intention to carry all of them to the shores of ultimate bliss. To practice Buddhism without making the vow to save all sentient beings is to leave out the most important part of the religion. It is like plowing a field and then forgetting to plant any seeds.

The Mahayana mind is often described as having three parts. The first part involves the bodhi mind, the second involves the compassionate mind, and the third involves the skillful mind. Master Taixu said that the awakened mind is the cause of the Mahayana vow, the compassionate mind is the basis and the skillful mind is the completion. The skillful mind is that part of us that tries to be effective in teaching others and leading them to the truth. All sentient beings are different, so we need to learn to use many skillful methods for helping them.

Many years ago Sariputra, who was on the verge of becoming enlightened, initiated the Mahayana mind. To test his resolve, a heavenly being came down to earth and pretended to be a child.

The child sat on the roadside where he knew that Sariputra would pass. As Sariputra neared, the child started crying. When Sariputra saw how sad the child was he asked him why he was crying. The child said that it was none of his business, and continued to cry.

Sariputra said, "I am a disciple of the Buddha. My deepest intent is to help others. Please tell me why you are feeling so sad."

The child said, "It's no use. There is nothing you can do to help."

Sariputra said, "Please tell me! Maybe I can help."

The child said, "My mother is ill and she is going to die. Her doctor said that the only way to save her is to make a medicine from the eye of a living saint. It is hard enough to obtain an eye from a living person. To get one from a saint is impossible!"

Sariputra said, "I will help you!"

The child said, "But how?"

Sariputra said, "I have dedicated my life to others, so in a way I could be called a saint. I am willing to do whatever I can to help others. You can have one of my eyes." With that he leaned toward the child and said, "Just pull out the one you want!"

The heavenly being who had been transformed into a child said, "Oh, I couldn't do that! I would be harming you! It would be better if you pull it out for me."

With that, Sariputra gouged out his left eye and handed it to the child, saying, "Here this is for your mother. I hope she gets well soon."

The child looked at Sariputra and said, "Oh no! You pulled out the wrong eye! I have to have your right eye! The left eye is not good for this kind of medicine."

With that, Sariputra gouged out his right eye and handed it to the child.

The child took the eye, but then suddenly said that it smelled bad and that he didn't want it. He threw it down on the ground and stomped on it. Then he yelled at Sariputra saying, "This eye stinks! How can you expect me to give something like this to my mother?"

Sariputra eventually became enlightened, but this story is a good reminder that the path is not always an easy one. The *Avatamsaka Sutra* contains a long passage explaining that sentient beings are mean, ungrateful, stupid, lazy, nasty, and rude and that if you are really serious about saving them, you must be prepared to be treated very badly. The Mahayana mind is not for weak spirits. It requires that we be ready and able to apply the Buddha's teachings to some very difficult situations. The Buddha taught that there are 84,000 kinds of delusion and that we therefore need to learn many skillful methods for helping others. A method that works well with one person, may not work well with another. When we vow to help others, we must bear in mind that the help that we provide needs to do some good. We are not being helpful when we use methods that do not succeed.

Our use of wise methods should be founded on what might be called "wise compassion." Compassion is an emotion, and it is based on our ability to empathize with others, and yet to be effective with others we must also use reason. If someone steps on a piece of glass, our emotions may tell us that it will hurt them to pull it out, but our reason will tell us that they will be hurt even more if we do not pull it out. Wise compassion means that we use both emotion and reason to understand the needs of others. If we really want to fulfill our Mahayana mind, we must learn how to communicate well. First we must listen, then we must think and feel deeply, then we can make a good decision. Most of the time most people just need to have us listen to them. Simply listening to others opens channels of compassion and wisdom that often do more to effect changes for the better than all other methods combined.

Do not be afraid of yourself. Learn who you are and then use your wisdom to help. No matter what you have done, your experiences can be used to help others as long as you have come to fully understand them yourself. Who better to help an alcoholic than a former alcoholic who has cured himself? Who better to help a young person with low self-esteem than someone who felt the same way at that age? There are 84,000 kinds of delusion. If you have succeeded in curing yourself of one or two of them, there will be someone who can benefit from your help.

When we help others, powerful forces always come into our lives to help us as well. While we may initiate the Mahayana mind for the first time, we should not forget that there are beings all over the universe who initiated this same mind eons ago. When we join their ranks, we will be noticeably empowered by their strength and by their concern for us. Our lives may not seem to change all that much at first, but if we are receptive, as time goes on we will learn to sense their presence, and to call on them for help. You are not alone. When you vow to help others, you join the greatest group of beings in the universe. Powerful forces will come to your aid because you have earned their respect, and because your intentions are directed toward goodness. When we turn away from our selfish and harmful attachments, we join with forces that are greater than anything we can imagine.

Once there was a novice monk who was walking with his master. The monk had been thinking about the Mahayana mind for days. At last he said, "Master I am ready to vow to dedicate my life to liberating all sentient beings in the universe."

His master was delighted. He turned to the young monk who was walking behind him and said, "Here, give me that heavy pack you are carrying. And please, now you must walk in front of me."

The young monk felt awkward but he did as he was told. He gave his heavy pack to his master and began strolling ahead with his arms swinging at his sides. After a few hours of this easy pace, he noticed a large ant hill on the side of the path. As he contemplated how many sentient beings there were in just that one ant hill, his resolve began to weaken. He thought to himself, "I don't think that I really do want to liberate all sentient beings in the universe for there are so very many of them. I should concentrate on liberating myself instead."

His master, who had considerable supernatural powers, heard his thoughts. The moment the young monk concluded that he would concentrate on liberating only himself, he said, "Here you can carry this heavy pack now. And it is time for you to walk behind me again."

When we are not committed to our goals, they rarely if ever are accomplished. When we are committed to our goals, powerful forces come to our aid. If our goals are wholesome and beneficial to others, there is nothing that can stop us from accomplishing them for our resolve will draw on the greatest source of energy in the universe. There is nothing stronger than a compassionate mind. And there is nothing greater than loving kindness. As we bow humbly before these gentle forces, we will discover that we are flooded with a strength that is greater than any other in the world.

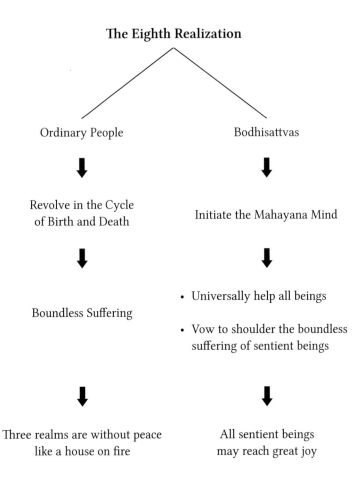

Chapter IX

Conclusion

These eight realizations are the realizations of all Buddhas and bodhisattvas. Diligently practice the Way and compassionately cultivate wisdom. Take the Great Dharma Vessel and reach the shore of nirvana, then return again to the cycle of birth and death to liberate sentient beings. Use these eight realizations to teach all beings and allow sentient beings to awaken to the suffering of the cycle of birth and death, turn away from the five desires, and cultivate the mind on the noble path. If a disciple of the Buddha recites these eight realizations in every thought he can eliminate boundless wrongdoings, progress towards bodhi, and quickly attain right enlightenment, forever cut off birth and death and always be happy.

Chapter Nine

Conclusion
Approaching the Awakened State

The Dharma teaches us how to "approach the awakened state." It does not simply give us this state. The concluding section of this sutra tells us that if we practice the suggestions made in the sutra, we will "quickly attain right enlightenment." Master Huangbo (?-850) was once asked, "Delusion blocks our view of the true mind; how are we to remove delusion from our minds?" The master replied, "Being deluded and removing delusion are the same thing because both of them only give rise to more delusion. In the deepest sense, delusion has no basis whatsoever. It arises out of how we think... When we succeed in being attached to neither the enlightened nor the unenlightened state, we will achieve the Buddha mind."

When a disciple asked Master Huangbo which was his true mind, the Buddha mind or the ordinary mind, Huangbo said, "How many minds do you think you have?"

How many minds do we have? All of the Buddha's teachings are directed at getting us to use our minds to see the one mind that resides in all things. Buddhist masters often speak in paradoxes because the only thing that prevents us from attaining the Buddha mind are the limitations of our minds. Enlightenment is often called "liberation" or "ultimate freedom" because it is a state that is beyond all confinement, all error, and all inner blockages. The *Eight Realizations of a Bodhisattva Sutra* is a short description of how to apply the teachings of the Buddha to the events of our lives. None of the techniques described in this sutra can be done for us. When the Buddha asks us to contemplate impermanence, he is asking us to understand a basic feature of our lives. When he asks us to contemplate that the five aggregates are empty, he is asking us to realize that the very foundation of our "individuality" is comprised of nothing but illusions. The deeper we allow ourselves to see this truth, the deeper our understanding of life will be, and the quicker our enlightenment will arrive. No one can see these things for us. We must do these contemplations ourselves.

Once there was a very devout Buddhist practitioner who walked to her temple every morning for services. One day, as she proceeded in the dim light of early dawn, her foot stepped on something. At the same time she heard a "croaking" noise under her shoe. Since it was still too dark to see what she had stepped on, the woman continued on her way to the temple. And yet as she walked, she felt terribly guilty for she was sure that she had just killed a small frog. Her guilt was compounded by her knowledge that the frog had been killed while she had been on her way to the temple. All during the morning service she felt sorrow for what she had done. On her way home, she examined the path with great care to see if she could find the frog and bury him properly. Then suddenly she saw the truth of what had happened—lying in the path were a couple of dry bean pods. She stepped gingerly on one of them and heard the sound that she had heard that morning. Greatly relieved, she hurried home to continue with her day's activities.

Sometimes we imagine that we have done something harmful when we have not, and sometimes we imagine that we have done something good when we have not. The teachings described in this sutra are intended to help us see beyond all delusions, all dualistic thinking, all illusory appearances of separation and individuality and the greed and fear that arise from these. Master Huangbo said, "If we are always thinking in terms of absolutes, then we are making a mistake. The way to end this mistake is to contemplate that all things are empty." The contemplation of emptiness helps us overcome all of the many delusions that lie among the dualities of this world. The woman who feared that she had stepped on a frog, worried herself needlessly by her mistake. Fortunately, she corrected herself by going back along the path and discovering what had really happened. Her return journey was like a contemplation that gave her the opportunity to re-examine her assumptions in the light of truth.

Life does not always allow us to go back along its paths to find out what really happened, but it does allow us to stop and think about the way our minds work, and the ways that we choose to conduct ourselves in this world. A Buddha is an awakened human being. The way to quickly become enlightened is to apply these teachings in your life.

佛說八大人覺經

The Eight Realizations of a Bodhisattva Sutra

佛 說 八 大 人 覺 經
Fo Shuo Ba Da Ren Jue Jing

為 佛 弟 子 。 常 於 晝 夜 。
Wei Fo Di Zi　 Chang Yu Zhou Ye

至 心 誦 念 。 八 大 人 覺 。
Zhi Xin Song Nian　 Ba Da Ren Jue

第 一 覺 悟 。 世 間 無 常 。
Di Yi Jue Wu　 Shi Jian Wu Chang

國 土 危 脆 。 四 大 苦 空 。
Guo Tu Wei Cui　 Si Da Ku Kong

五 陰 無 我 。 生 滅 變 異 。
Wu Yin Wu Wo　 Sheng Mie Bian Yi

虛 偽 無 主 。 心 是 惡 源 。
Xu Wei Wu Zhu　 Xin Shi E Yuan

形 為 罪 藪 。 如 是 觀 察 。
Xing Wei Zui Sou　 Ru Shi Guan Cha

漸 離 生 死 。
Jian Li Sheng Si

第 二 覺 知。 多 欲 為 苦。
Di Er Jue Zhi   Duo Yu Wei Ku

生 死 疲 勞。 從 貪 欲 起。
Sheng Si Pi Lao   Cong Tan Yu Qi

少 欲 無 為。 身 心 自 在。
Shao Yu Wu Wei   Shen Xin Zi Zai

第 三 覺 知。 心 無 厭 足。
Di San Jue Zhi   Xin Wu Yan Zu

唯 得 多 求。 增 長 罪 惡。
Wei De Duo Qiu   Zeng Zhang Zui E

菩 薩 不 爾。 常 念 知 足。
Pu Sa Bu Er   Chang Nian Zhi Zu

安 貧 守 道。 唯 慧 是 業。
An Pin Shou Dao   Wei Hui Shi Ye

第 四 覺 知。 懈 怠 墜 落。
Di Si Jue Zhi   Xie Dai Duo Luo

常 行 精 進。 破 煩 惱 惡。
Chang Xing Jing Jin   Po Fan Nao E

摧　伏　四　魔　。　出　陰　界　獄　。
Cui　Fu　Si　Mo　。　Chu　Yin　Jie　Yu　。

第　五　覺　悟　。　愚　癡　生　死　。
Di　Wu　Jue　Wu　。　Yu　Chi　Sheng　Si　。

菩　薩　常　念　。　廣　學　多　聞　。
Pu　Sa　Chang　Nian　。　Guang　Xue　Duo　Wen　。

增　長　智　慧　。　成　就　辯　才　。
Zeng　Zhang　Zhi　Hui　。　Cheng　Jiu　Bian　Cai　。

教　化　一　切　。　悉　以　大　樂　。
Jiao　Hua　Yi　Qie　。　Xi　Yi　Da　Le　。

第　六　覺　知　。　貧　苦　多　怨　。
Di　Liu　Jue　Zhi　。　Pin　Ku　Duo　Yuan　。

橫　結　惡　緣　。　菩　薩　布　施　。
Heng　Jie　E　Yuan　。　Pu　Sa　Bu　Shi　。

等　念　冤　親　。　不　念　舊　惡　。
Deng　Nian　Yuan　Qin　。　Bu　Nian　Jiu　E　。

不　憎　惡　人　。
Bu　Zeng　E　Ren　。

第七覺悟。五欲過患。
Di Qi Jue Wu   Wu Yu Guo Huan

雖為俗人。不染世樂。
Sui Wei Su Ren   Bu Ran Shi Le

常念三衣。瓦鉢法器。
Chang Nian San Yi   Wa Bo Fa Qi

志願出家。守道清白。
Zhi Yuan Chu Jia   Shou Dao Qing Bai

梵行高遠。慈悲一切。
Fan Heng Gao Yuan   Ci Bei Yi Qie

第八覺知。生死熾然。
Di Ba Jue Zhi   Sheng Si Chi Ran

苦惱無量。發大乘心。
Ku Nao Wu Liang   Fa Da Sheng Xin

普濟一切。願代眾生。
Pu Ji Yi Qie   Yuan Dai Zhong Sheng

受無量苦。令諸眾生。
Shou Wu Liang Ku   Ling Zhu Zhong Sheng

畢 竟 大 樂 。
Bi Jing Da Le

如 此 八 事 。 乃 是 諸 佛
Ru Ci Ba Shi Nai Shi Zhu Fo

菩 薩 大 人 之 所 覺 悟 。
Pu Sa Da Ren Zhi Suo Jue Wu

精 進 行 道 慈 悲 修 慧 。
Jing Jin Xing Dao Ci Bei Xiu Hui

乘 法 身 船 至 涅 槃 岸 。
Cheng Fa Sheng Chuan zhi Nie Pan An

復 還 生 死 度 脫 眾 生 。
Fu Huan Shen Si Du Tuo Zhong Sheng

以 前 八 事 。 開 導 一 切 。
Yi Qian Ba Shi Kai Dao Yi Qie

令 諸 眾 生 覺 生 死 苦 。
Ling Zhu Zhong Sheng Jue Sheng Si Ku

捨 離 五 欲 修 心 聖 道 。
She Li Wu Yu Xiu Xin Sheng Dao

若 佛 弟 子 。 誦 此 八 事 。
Ruo Fo Di Zi　Song Ci Ba Shi

於 念 念 中 。 滅 無 量 罪 。
Yu Nian Nian Zhong　Mie Wu Liang Zui

進 趣 菩 提 。 速 登 正 覺 。
Jin Qu Pu Ti　Shu Deng Zheng Jue

永 斷 生 死 。 常 住 快 樂 。
Yong Duan Sheng Si　Chang Zhu Kuai Le

About the Author

Founder of the Fo Guang Shan (Buddha's Light Mountain) Buddhist Order and the Buddha's Light International Association, Venerable Master Hsing Yun has dedicated his life to teaching Humanistic Buddhism, which seeks to realize spiritual cultivation in everyday living.

Master Hsing Yun is the 48th Patriarch of the Linji Chan School. Born in Jiangsu Province, China in 1927, he was tonsured under Venerable Master Zhikai at the age of twelve and became a novice monk at Qixia Vinaya College. He was fully ordained in 1941 following years of strict monastic training. When he left Jiaoshan Buddhist College at the age of twenty, he had studied for almost ten years in a monastery.

Due to the civil war in China, Master Hsing Yun moved to Taiwan in 1949 where he undertook the revitalization of Chinese Mahayana Buddhism. He began fulfilling his vow to promote the Dharma by starting chanting groups, student and youth groups, and other civic-minded organizations with Leiyin Temple in Ilan as his base. Since the founding of Fo Guang Shan monastery in Kaohsiung in 1967, more than two hundred temples have been established worldwide. Hsi Lai Temple, the symbolic torch of the Dharma spreading to the West, was built in 1988 near Los Angeles.

Master Hsing Yun has been guiding Buddhism on a course of modernization by integrating Buddhist values into education, cultural activities, charity, and religious practices. To achieve these ends, he travels all over the world, giving lectures and actively engaging in religious dialogue. The Fo Guang Shan organization also oversees sixteen Buddhist colleges and four universities, one of which is the University of the West in Rosemead, California.

Other Works by Venerable Master Hsing Yun:

The Rabbit's Horn
A Commentary on the Platform Sutra

For All Living
A Guide to Buddhist Practice

Infinite Compassion, Endless Wisdom
The Practice of the Bodhisattva Path

Between Ignorance and Enlightenment

Where is Your Buddha Nature?
Stories to Instruct and Inspire

Being Good
Buddhist Ethics for Everyday Life

Chan Heart, Chan Art

Sutra of the Medicine Buddha
With an Introduction, Comments, and Prayers

The Core Teachings

About Buddha's Light Publishing

As long as Venerable Master Hsing Yun has been a Buddhist monk, he has had a strong belief that books and other documentation of the Buddha's teachings unite us emotionally, help us practice Buddhism at a higher level, and continuously challenge our views on how we define our lives.

In 1996, the Fo Guang Shan International Translation Center was established with this goal in mind. This marked the beginning of a string of publications translated into various languages from the Master's original writings in Chinese. Presently, several translation centers have been set up worldwide. Centers that coordinate translation or publication projects are located in Los Angeles and San Diego, USA; Sydney, Australia; Berlin, Germany; Argentina; South Africa; and Japan.

In 2001, Buddha's Light Publishing was established to publish Buddhist books translated by the Fo Guang Shan International Translation Center as well as other valuable Buddhist works. Buddha's Light Publishing is committed to building bridges between East and West, Buddhist communities, and cultures. All proceeds from our book sales support Buddhist propagation efforts.